KILL? FOR PEACE?

Richard McSorley, S.J.

CENTER FOR PEACE STUDIES

Rm #2 O'Gara Building
Georgetown University
Washington, D.C. 20057

KILL? FOR PEACE? is a publication of the Center for Peace Studies. The Center works to integrate Faith, Action and Research into the process of peace.

The Center for Peace Studies offers resources for peace teaching including slide shows, tapes, printed material, taped lectures, and resource people to develop peace themes to supplement the work of interested groups and teachers.

First published 1970
Revised 1977

Library of Congress Catalog Card Number: 70-135455

Table of Contents

Chapter 1

NUCLEAR DISASTER

One of the best kept secrets of our day is the amount of disaster that nuclear weapons can produce. It may seem strange to call it "secret" when there are so many books that tell its story, books like Tom Stonier's *Nuclear Disaster* and Norman Cousin's *In Place of Folly,* the Atomic Energy Hearings of 1959, and the United Nations Task Force Report on Nuclear Arms Escalation.

Yet it is kind of secret, an open secret. The information is available and is not too hard to understand, but both the government and the military block information rather than help provide it. The man on the street does not know what nuclear weapons can do. This is evidence enough to show that the secret is being kept. Ask the man on the street: "What would a twenty-megaton weapon do if dropped on New York City? A one-megaton? What is a megaton?"

One way the military tries to keep the secret is to accuse those who stir up fear of nuclear weapons of aiding the communists. Another is to classify the material so that it is not open to public discussion.

I once invited an Undersecretary of Defense to speak to my class. I asked him especially to point out the destructive capacity of bombs of various sizes. He replied that any information giving a norm or measure by which the destructive capacity could be gauged was considered classified (secret). I told him that the information is readily available in public books; he simply repeated that it was classified. He was speaking to an audience that already had the information, but he would not discuss or confirm that information. This is secrecy directed against citizens and not at any enemy.

In England, the government blocked the British Broadcasting System from showing the film *War Games* on television. The reason given was that if the people saw, in a realistic way, the disaster that might come from a small nuclear attack, the shock might be too great for them. The truth was probably that the government feared that the people might rise up against the continued manufacture of these weapons if they realized what horrible destruction they could cause.

The same reason, I think, explains the classification of information about the amount of damage that nuclear weapons can do. If we seriously considered the destructive force of nuclear weapons, we would not look on them as a way to securing peace. This would be a big change in our thinking. Einstein noted this. He said: "The splitting of the atom has changed everything save our modes of thinking and thus we drift toward unparalleled catastrophe."

To understand the power of nuclear weapons, compare them with the big bombs of World War II. A World War II blockbuster was the equivalent of a ton of TNT in explosive force. A large air raid was equivalent to 1,000 tons of TNT. An entire air raid like that is twenty times smaller than the small nuclear weapon dropped on Hiroshima, since that bomb was equivalent to 20,000 tons the Hiroshima bomb is a baby in the atomic weapon family.

The Hiroshima bomb size has to be multiplied by fifty to equal the size of a one-megaton bomb. "Megaton" is one of the new words coined to describe a million tons of TNT equivalent, and megatonage has no theoretical upper limit.

The early H-bomb in 1952 was a three-megaton weapon, the equivalent of three million tons of TNT in destructive power. A later H-bomb tested by the Soviet Union in 1961 was 57 megatons. It is difficult to imagine what this means: The strength of such an H-bomb is equivalent to the explosive power of a 1,000-ton World War II air raid continued every day for 156 years!

When you consider that these weapons can be carried in airplanes traveling faster than sound, delivered in missiles or from submarines that remain at the bottom of the sea, the dimension of danger increases. Some idea of what a nuclear war would be like can be obtained by looking at what one weapon can destroy. Multiply that destruction by the number of weapons likely to be used. This gives you a picture of the basic destruction likely in World War III.

What would a twenty-megaton nuclear bomb do if it exploded in the heart of New York City? It is important to consider the bomb in relation to a city for two reasons. First, the likely target of these bombs is cities. Second, 80 per cent of the American people live in cities. We are an urban population. It is an irony of fate that the most urban population in the world has developed the weapons that can destroy cities. The first result of a twenty-megaton bomb dropped on midtown Manhattan would be death. "The total number of people killed would be about ten times the total number of battle deaths that the United States has suffered throughout all its history, that is, from the American Revolution through Vietnam."[1] The estimated deaths would be six million of New York's eight million people and another million dead beyond the city limits.

If you took a road map of New York City and drew circles on it to indicate the blast area, the fire storm area, and the radiation area, you could draw a circle with a radius extending ten miles from the explosion center to indicate the lethal blast area. Beyond this, a larger circle with a radius extending thirty-seven miles from the center would mark off the area of the fire storm. The radiation area would not be a circle because the radiation would blow with the wind and form a parabolic, or long cigar-shaped area.

BLAST EFFECT

A twenty-megaton bomb has "more destructive power than a mountain of TNT four times the height of the Empire State Building . . .more . . . than a caravan of one million trucks each carrying 20,000 pounds of TNT." [2] Its blast would make a hole in solid rock deep enough to contain a twenty-story building; and the hole would be half a mile wide. The detonation would set a huge pressure wave in motion. This would roar out from the explosion center as a shock front backed by winds moving at over 1,000 miles per hour.

Behind the pressure front, a vast vacuum would be created. Into this, the winds from the surrounding area would rush as the pressure diminished. Structures not smashed by the shock front might be toppled by the winds sucked in by the vacuum from the opposite direction.

Most casualties in New York City would come from falling buildings and flying objects. Some people would be killed by being blown against walls and hard objects. "Trucks would be lifted and thrown like grotesque

Molotov cocktails to spew gasoline, oil and automotive shrapnel onto and into everything in their path. In an instant, most underground gasoline and oil tanks would rupture and explode within the blast area."[3]

Within a ten-mile radius from the center, the area of lethal or severe blast, basement shelters would be buried. All living things in the subway systems would die. Frame houses and two-story brick buildings would be destroyed. "Few, if any, of New York City's approximately 2,500,000 dwelling units would provide adequate shelter for survivors, even if everything were not consumed by fires."[4]

The blast would destroy hospitals, rupture water mains, and paralyze transportation. The winds from the blast would fan the fury of the fires to follow it.

FIRESTORM

After the incandescent flash across the sky, a fireball as hot as the sun and many times brighter would begin to rise from the earth. It would be four and a half miles across. Like a hot air balloon, it would rise to a height of twenty miles, emitting visible and invisible radiation and scorching the countryside. Clothing on people twenty miles away would burst into flame; paper and similar material would pass their combustion point at thirty-seven miles. "People about 40 miles away could suffer first degree burns."[5]

A sea of fire would roll and burn within a radius extending thirty-seven miles from the center. And as far away as 300 miles from the blast center retinal damage might be inflicted on those who looked at the fire wall. (Rabbits at that distance from the U.S. Pacific tests of smaller bombs had their eyes burned by the flash of the bomb.) Closer to the fire center less combustible materials like asphalt would blaze.

RADIATION

Blast effects and even some of the fireball effects are familiar from past wars. Their size and power are increased with nuclear weapons. Radiation effect, however, is entirely new and different.

A ground burst gives off more radioactive fallout than an air burst. The reason is that the material in the crater created by the blast is vaporized, and the same is true of many objects touched by the fireball. In the case of a twenty-megaton bomb dropped on New York City, the crater would be over 600 feet deep and 1½ miles across. The vaporized material would be carried into the upper atmosphere and then fall according to wind currents as radioactive particles. The heavy material falls first, the lighter drifts farther before falling to the ground.

Radiation damage may result from exposure to these particles. Long-range injury is incurred by the body's becoming a depository of radioactive materials. Radiation damage is measured in roentgen units. One roentgen is enough to damage human cells. The number of roentgens necessary to kill 50 per cent of the humans exposed is 450 roentgens.

Large doses of 2,000 or 3,000 roentgens kill by paralyzing the central nervous system. Doses of about 1,500 roentgens kill by producing fatal gastrointestinal disorders. Below 1,500 units the roentgen dosage affects the blood system. It decreases the oxygen, white blood cells, and the ability of the blood to clot. This may explain blue or purple patches beneath the skin of radiation patients.

Fallout from a twenty-megaton ground burst on New York City would cover an area of about 4,800 square miles depending on the wind. If the wind blew east, this would include Connecticut and the Cape Cod area. In this area the roentgen dosage would be 2,100 units by the end of the second day and then would decline. During these two days exposed persons would probably die. But the air would remain lethal to 50 per cent of the population for at least the next twelve days, perhaps for as long as two months. For twelve days the dosage would be 575 roentgens. Afterward it would decline, but one hundred roentgens would continue to exist during the next ten months.

The only way that the population could adequately protect itself would be to have three feet of dirt or two feet of concrete between itself and the radiation for the period of danger. Even if that were possible, relief operations would be completely impeded. Any attempt to repair power lines or water mains, to put out fires, or to give medical care would expose the relief crew to lethal fallout during the first two weeks, with lesser fallout thereafter.

Superficial radiation burns resulting from sublethal doses make a person more vulnerable to diseases and lessen his ability to recover from injury. Alone they are not serious; neither are minor injuries. Combined with other injuries or the lack of medical attention, however, they can be fatal or cause permanent damage.

Radioactive material is deposited within the bone structure of the body when one breathes contaminated air or eats and drinks radioactive material. This was vividly illustrated in the British tests. The antlers of a deer and the teeth of a sheep became so radioactive that they printed their own image on a photographic plate. The deposit of radioactive strontium 90 and caesium 137 caused the bone structure to act like an internal X-ray machine.

How long contamination from eating or drinking radioactive materials may last can be judged by the United States Navy's announcement of August 11, 1968, that Bikini Atoll is now fit for human habitation. The Navy conducted tests on Bikini in 1946. These carefully limited tests made the atoll unsafe for human life for twenty-two years.

Those who survived a ground burst of a heavy nuclear device would be living for weeks, if they lived at all, in a radioactive oven. Every responsible scientist admits that fallout of large megatonage would leave us with an appalling number of deformities that could continue for many generations. A general nuclear war would leave us with hundreds of millions of cripples, idiots, and invalids.

LESSER BOMBS

I have concentrated attention on the twenty-megaton weapon since that is a medium-sized one between the one-megaton and the fifty-seven megaton weapons which are within our capacity for use. Similar charts of the circle of destruction of a one-megaton or a ten-megaton blast could easily be laid out. Their destructive capacity is still immense. Twenty bombs of one-megaton size would do more proportionate damage than one twenty-megaton bomb. For example, each one-megaton would have a blast area of three to four miles in radius (compared with the ten-mile blast radius of the twenty-megaton bomb); a firestorm area three to nine miles in radius (compared with the twenty-seven-miles for the twenty megaton); and radiation that would start over the six- to eighteen-mile diameter of the firestorm and blow 200 miles with the wind (compared with the 4,800-square-mile radiation area for a twenty-megaton bomb). In addition the "ones" could be placed according to density of population; the "twenty" would have to hit a single target. The "ones" could be exploded both on the ground and in the air over the same target, or on different targets. The effects of air and ground bursts are different. Air bursts produce 30 to 40 per cent more blast and fire damage than ground bursts. A ground burst gives off much more radiation.

JAPAN, 1945

Instead of circles and statistics, the effect of nuclear weapons on people tells a more effective story of their destructive power in human terms.

After the markets were open at Hiroshima and the people were on their way to work, a single atom bomb was dropped from a high altitude. The bomb measured only 28 inches by 128 inches. It floated down on a parachute. At 1,804 feet above the ground, it exploded. A picture taken shortly after the explosion shows the devastation: charred human bodies on a desert of wreckage. Our country's official report estimates that 66,000 people were killed and 69,000 were injured. Other reports put the number of dead closer to 100,000. All this killing in a few minutes!

With this act we became the first nation to drop an atomic weapon on human beings. This was done despite the plea of a group of scientists to President Truman that we should not be the first to do this. The argument is sometimes given that we killed all those people and injured almost twice as many in order to save lives and bring the war to an end. But this rationalization is without merit.

We could have starved the Japanese war machine by interfering with its supply of fuel. We could have waited! Germany had already surrendered. Victory was assured. In fact, as Philip Berrigan points out in his book *A Punishment for Peace*, President Truman acted against the advice of the best military and civilian leaders in both England and the United States. Those who advised against the use of the bomb included General Eisenhower, Churchill, and the U.S. Joint Chiefs of Staff—except General Marshall. [6]

The argument that dropping the bomb was necessary to

force Japan into ending the war is simply contrary to the facts.

Japan was already asking for peace. One faction in Japan was demanding that its government end the war. Whatever rationalization we might have made for the destruction of Hiroshima was weakened when, three days later, we fried Nagasaki in a nuclear flash.

On August 9 at 11:02 P.M. another B-29 dropped a bomb on the industrial section of Nagasaki, totally destroying the city, killing 39,000 persons and injuring 25,000 more. This was our report. Other estimates put the casualties higher. A general rule of thumb is that for each death there are twice that number of casualties.

After the detonation, the devastation made Nagasaki look like incinerated Hiroshima. Our argument that we were trying to save lives now seems hollow and empty: Before we weighed the effects of the first bomb and while Japan was still trying to assess it, we struck again. The bombs of Nagasaki and Hiroshima gave us an incarnate example of what the bomb can do to a city.

These were small bombs on relatively small cities, but their effect on the people of Japan, even today, is to make them adverse to any military cooperation with the United States and afraid of the same thing happening again. This is the reason why mass protests against American nuclear installations in Japan and against cooperation with the United States in Vietnam strike a resonant chord in the hearts of most Japanese. They have felt the terror of atomic destruction.

OVERKILL CAPACITY

Now we have a basic estimate of the damage that can be done with a single nuclear weapon. Multiply this destruction by the number of weapons that both we and the Soviet Union possess and you can get a realistic estimate of what these weapons could do.

How many weapons does the United States have? In February of 1968, Secretary McNamara said the United States had 4,500 nuclear warheads. Of these, 656 were ready to be launched from nuclear-powered submarines. The Soviet Union had 1,000 nuclear warheads. Secretary McNamara also pointed out with a chart that a total of 400 megatons is all that is needed to destroy 76 per cent of any enemy's industrial capacity. He showed from his table that increasing the number of megatons four times would only increase the amount of industrial capacity destroyed by 1 per cent. [7]

In other words, with 400 megatons as the breakoff point for deterring any aggressor, we have ten times more megatons than we need. This is something new in warfare. It used to be that the way to win a war was to develop more or bigger weapons than the enemy. Now we both have such weapons and so many more than we need that no deterrent advantage comes from more or bigger weapons. In fact, the development of bigger weapons might provoke nuclear war on the part of the power unable to develop more weapons.

"Overkill" is the word that expresses this. It tells of a frustration at the limits of power ("how many times can you kill a man?")—frustration because "more power" is no longer the program for victory.

At the SALT (Strategic Arms Limitation) talk of May 1972, we admitted we had 5,792 warheads ready to go. By the time the SALT agreement ends in 1977, we will have 10,213; the Soviet Union will have 3,869. By 1980 we will have 16,200 deliverable warheads. This does not include all we have. The world stockpile of nuclear weapons is over 50,000 megatons of which we have more than half. Yet we continue to make a new nuclear weapon every eight hours.

Another way of understanding the 400 megatons delivered on the enemy as the outside limit of deterrence is this. The Soviet Union has approximately 200 cities with a population of 100,000 or over. If we delivered one nuclear weapon on each of these cities we would devastate the country and its industrial capacity. Actually McNamara spoke of 200 to 400. It is this 200 figure that President Carter used in 1977 when he asked Defense Secretary Brown to look into the possibility of the United States reducing its nuclear force to 200 to 400 megatons all carried in submarines.

WAR OF MANY H-BOMBS

In 1959 a Congressional Committee held hearings on the effects of a war of many H-bombs. They spent a week on testimony about what would happen if 263 H-bombs with a total of 1,446 megatons of explosive force hit targets in the United States. That would be less than one-tenth of our present stockpile megatonage. The result was calculated to be 50 million dead and 20 million seriously wounded.

Senator Robert F. Kennedy put it more clearly. In a Senate speech, June 23, 1965, he said: "Eighty million Americans—and hundreds of million of other people would die within the first 24 hours of a full-scale nuclear exchange . . . the survivors would envy the dead." He was repeating what President John F. Kennedy had said in his 1961 speech before the United Nations.

A United Nations Task Force report agrees with their estimate. It says:

It can be calculated that a hypothetical attack of 10,000 megatons in ground bursts, could, in the course of 60 days, destroy 80% of the population of the United States if unprotected, while an ttack of 20,000 megatons could cover the entire country with adioactive fallout, killing 95% of the unprotected population. [10]

The massiveness of the destruction cannot be grasped merely by statistics of the dead and wounded. The disaster would be so great that the spirit of man might be paralyzed into coma for decades.

What would it be like when a whole country or two great nations were destroyed as viable societies? Those who survived would certainly judge that the destruction was not worth the result. One thing seems certain to me: nothing we recognize as our free institutions would survive. This is why the literature of nuclear destruction has the recurrent theme "the survivors will envy the dead." I think they would.

AFTEREFFECTS OF NUCLEAR WAR

We can make some calculations on what the after-effects would be. The massiveness of the destruction would leave medical problems unsolved and insoluble; the absence of water, housing, and food would make the struggle to recover a nightmare; the disruption of the social and economic structure of society is almost unimaginable. These effects would be somewhat familiar from other wars, but the size of the disaster would be so enormous that a totally new situation would confront us. Sterility and senescence would be caused by the radiation, which would especially affect the generative process. Imbalances between plants, insects, and animals because of radiation and general destruction would bring on pestilences and plagues that would not be checked by ordinary means. Soil erosion would continue to the third and fourth generation as a result of the destruction.

As an example of the difficulty of recovery after nuclear attack, imagine a truck driver faced with a rescue job. Ordinarily he takes orders from an employer and expects a pay-check to go through a bank. The bank may be destroyed and his employer dead. He is worried about his own family. They are far away and he cannot reach them. He is uncertain of the contamination level if he were to drive into an area. He might be attacked on the way for his supplies. He does not know whether he would be caught in another nuclear attack if he were to venture outside.

This person would face psychological and social difficulties that man has never faced before. Could he be depended upon to take part in a rescue team, or would he, like the people who survived the Hiroshima blast, stand dazed and paralyzed by it all and wonder whether it were worth trying to begin again?

This is just a basic summary of how the power of the atom and the development of technology have changed war. No longer is it what it used to be: something man could experiment with and not be hurt very much. The word *war* no longer means what it used to mean. _National suicide_ would be a better word than *war* for nuclear conflict.

What morality and love have never accomplished, the end of wars, may now be forced on us by technology. To know the basic destructive power of nuclear weapons is a first step toward peace. It is with knowledge of that destructive power and the defenselessness of any nation against it that President John F. Kennedy put before the world the alternatives that face us: "Together we shall save our planet or together we shall perish in its flames."

A knowledge of the destructive power of nuclear weapons alone would confirm the truth of these statements. That is why everyone should be informed about the atomic arsenal. When "the poor man's nuclear weapons," chemical and biological means for destruction, are added, the horizons of horror grow wider.

CHEMICAL-BIOLOGICAL DESTRUCTION

In a class I taught at Georgetown in 1969, I showed the British Broadcasting Company (BBC) film "A Plague Upon Your Children." One result was that a student in the class who was preparing for medical school came to tell me that he had known in general that chemical-biological agents were being manufactured by the United States, yet he had no idea that it was so serious. He had not believed that we ever intended to use the weapons or that we were putting so much money and effort into it. He was surprised by the enormous power of these weapons.

After this student had seen the film and read SeymourHersch's *Chemical and Biological Warfare,* he wondered if he really wanted to go into medicine. He had chosen medicine as a profession exempt from killing. He had seen it as the very opposite of killing—the profession dedicated to the protection and development of human life. Now he was not so sure. What he had seen was public health in reverse.

The film shows the British laboratory at Porton, England. It starts with the outside of the building, showing the security around it. Then the film moves inside to explain the process of the manufacture of nerve gas. You see the technician pouring chemicals. You hear the announcer describe how cheap and simple it is to make weapons with such powerful destructive capacity.

Germany began the manufacture of nerve gas at the end of World War I. After the war, both the United States and Britain obtained help from German scientists in developing it.

Today, the United States Army has developed *GB*, a big "improvement" on the original German Gas. *GB attacks the central nervous system by blocking the action of a key enzyme, acetylcholinasterase (ACHE).* When this nerve gas enters, the body loses control over its muscle action and "strangles in its own vital organs." Seymour Hersh describes the effect of nerve gas poisoning as follows:

The voluntary muscles go into a state of vibration and then become paralyzed. With the involuntary muscles, which power the blood vessels and other internal organs, the delicate balance of actuating and deactuating nervous stimulations is upset. The pupils, bladder and alimentary canal constrict, the penis erects, the tear and saliva glands secrete and the heart slows. The cause of death is generally asphyxia following paralysis of the respiratory muscles. [11]

Death can come in less than a minute and, according to the Army Training Manual, "Military Chemistry and Chemical Agents": "Individuals poisoned by *GB* display approximately the same sequence of symptoms regardless of the route by which the poison enters the body." This can be by breathing the gas, absorbing it through the skin, or ingesting it with food or water.

GB is only one of the agents prepared in the laboratory. Virulent strains of known contagious diseases are developed. "Resistance to remedies" is the major characteristic that scientists seek to strengthen in these biological agents.

The United States spends over $650 million a year for research on chemical-biological war (CBW). This is almost four times what the country spends on cancer research. It is almost twice the figure first given to Congressman Richard McCarthy (D-New York) when he tried to get figures on it. It amounts to about $2 million per day. The army alone "operates six full-time CBW installations, employs more than 14,000 men and spends more than

$500 million a year on CBW.''[12] Nerve gas is produced at the Rocky Mountain arsenal near Denver and at a plant in Newport, Indiana. Edgewood arsenal near Baltimore is a major research facility of poisonous gases. Its budget in 1969 was $420 million. The main production plant for biological death is at Pine Bluff, Arkansas; the arsenal of Dugway Proving grounds, eighty miles south of Salt Lake City, is the main testing center.

Nerve gas came to public attention in 1968 when 6,400 sheep were killed near Dugway. First the army denied there was any testing; then under Congressional questioning it turned out that the army had lied and, confronted with evidence, was forced to admit that it was indeed testing nerve gas and that a tragedy had occurred.

The shipment of train loads of lethal chemicals across the country from Rocky Mountain Arsenal through New Jersey to the Atlantic Ocean for disposal aroused such public protest that the idea of transporting them was abandoned. Before the public outcry, the army had secretly made many shipments.

The effect of these weapons is phenomenal. The army's ''improved'' nerve gas, *GB*, will kill a man in thirty seconds. One-fiftieth of a drop on the back of the hand is enough. A small fraction of a drop on the eyeball is enough. The BBC film showed how it works on rabbits: paralysis, convulsions, vomiting, coma, and death. An aerosol spray of *GB* along the side of a field will kill all the horses in the field as the wind blows it on them.

GB is odorless, tasteless, and invisible. It can be spread in the form of poison clouds over large areas. The clouds can be created by missile release, by submarines, by planes, or by an ordinary tanker. Aerosol generators can quickly cover miles of ground or air with blankets of invisible death. It can be delivered in artillery shells, mortars, grenades, and rockets. It contaminates ground, air, and plants. A slight sniff of it or a drop on the skin means death.

The United States ships *GB* in containers all over the world to have it ready whenever and wherever we decide to use it.

The BBC film showed a simulated British Army maneuver where troops were under attack by nerve gas. The soldiers were totally covered by overalls and special helmets fitted with gas masks. Each soldier must wear a helmet and give himself an injection of a remedy called atropine before the gas reaches him or it is too late. In the film the simulated gas was visible. In real war it would be invisible. Unless you had your helmet on and had taken the injection before the gas reached you, you would be helpless: death would come too soon.

The film shows a tank coming to a stop after a nerve gas attack. As a soldier gets out, the announcer explains that, before returning to the tank, he would have to completely discard his outside clothes which had been contaminated by touching the air and he would have to put on new clothes. He does this by decontaminating the ground with a powder—he also must decontaminate his shoes with this powder. He then steps out of the overalls and unfolds a new pair which he puts on. He also dons new gloves. The film does not explain, as the narrator noted, how—in a gas attack—a man would be able to eat, to bring anything from inside a tin can to his mouth, unless he were already inside a sealed tank.

After this exhibit, the official spokesman for Britain said that, when the simulated operations were finished, a government report expressed confidence that British soldiers could operate satisfactorily under gas attack condition.

When the students in my class heard this, they laughed. It seemed quite ridiculous after what they had just seen. It also brought up the question "What happens to the civilian population?" Civilians would not have all this protection!

The film showed surgical operations performed under gas attack conditions. These required a completely sealed tent filled with oxygen. They required that the patient receive oxygen from the very moment that he was reached on the battlefield, which could only be a few seconds after the attack. The narrator mentioned that the surgical operation could proceed inside the tent provided there was no leak. However, it would be unsafe even with a single bullet hole. Then the tent would become infected with the gas.

The Commander of the Rocky Mountain Arsenal in 1954, Lt. Col. S.J. Efnor, describes *GB*'s capacity to kill: "The gas from a single bomb the size of a quart fruit jar could kill every living thing within a cubic mile, depending on the wind and weather condition . . ."[13] This agrees with other estimates.

In the summer of 1969, a group of scientists living in Denver protested the army's policy of storing nerve gas in steel cylinders located only two miles away from Stapleton Airport, the main airport for the city. They estimated that the cylinders held enough nerve gas to kill 100 billion people. Since there are only three billion people in the world, there is enough to kill each living person 33 times!

GERMS

In biological war the weapon is contagious disease; the ammunition is germs. Normally they travel into the lungs or blood system of man through the air from sources of infection. Germ warfare aims to develop a supply of germs that will be resistant to remedy and easily released against people the government thinks we should kill. However, as one scientist pointed out, germ warfare is "discriminate." It goes after people and does not harm property!

The main research center in the United States used to

be at Fort Detrick, Maryland, which housed 500 scientists who labored in secrecy. In 1973 some of them were moved to Utah. The scientists included 120 Ph.D.'s and 14 MD's. They work at producing resistant strains of diseases like anthrax, the black death of the Middle Ages. It kills up to 99 per cent of its victims. Tularemia, Q fever, typhus, encephalitis, cholera, smallpox, diphtheria, and brucellosis are some of the other diseases. These are tested on animals—a half million animals a year, mostly mice and rabbits.

None of the animals tested ever leave the place alive. Their bodies are incinerated. The danger of infection from the smoke of their burning bodies is so great that a high intensity oxygen furnace near the top of the smokestacks purifies the smoke as it passes out into the countryside.

Even with all the precautions, sterilization, special suits, and air conditioning, employees at the Fort sometimes die of exotic diseases. In 1965 Dr. Arthur N. Gorelick, head of the microbiological lab at Detrick, told Congress that since the lab opened in 1956, twelve workers had contracted diseases from their work. He added: "Many of the agents with which we are working are exotic . . . . There are usually no vaccines for preventing the disease nor drugs for treatment."[14] One of the victims, Albert Nickel, died of Venezuelan equine encephalitis on February 10, 1964.

According to one Fort Detrick study, there were a total of 3,330 laboratory accidents from 1954 to 1962. This included 410 people suffering from infections like brucellosis, tularemia, anthrax, and pneumonic plague. The plague victim, 22-year-old Ralph Powell, was handled so secretly and carelessly in 1959 that his presence risked the health of a neighboring city.

The BBC film showed how germs are multipled by painting them onto a culture pan and keeping them at body temperature. Other germs were injected into fertile eggs. Here the germ multiplies as much as 12 million times in a week. Small pox, encephalitis, and typhus are multiplied in this way.

After the multiplication process, the germs are removed and put into a liquid. From the liquid the germs can be aerosolized and sprayed into the air for testing on animals or they can be concentrated into a paste. One ounce of concentrated paste can contain 3 trillion germs. Eight ounces of paste would be enough to infect the entire world with a disease if properly diffused.

It is this miniature size plus the relative cheapness of manufacture that makes germ warfare available to poor nations. Any nation able to produce the fermentation for a beer brewery has enough biological equipment to begin a germ warfare plant.

In wartime, the human body becomes the culture in which the germs multiply. The germs multiply in the person, make him sick, perhaps kill him, and spread on to the next victim.

Sprayed in a cloud, the germs actually seek out the hidden person. They reach him in his shelter or through his contact with another person. How far the disease will go under man-made-plague conditions no one can tell. There is no natural defense or limit to the contagion. Such barriers have been broken by the massive contamination of the atmosphere and the massive infecting of people.

In a CBS film, General Rothschild, formerly head of the U.S. Army Chemical Corps, shows how a boat sailing along the west coast of Britain could spray clouds of germs that would blanket the British Isles and even drift into Europe. Until the population began to come down with the disease, no one would know they had been attacked. "The infection of an entire continent by biological clouds is possible under proper meterological conditions," says LeRoy D. Fothergill, special advisor to the U.S. Army Biological Laboratory.[15]

For the United States to lead the world in this kind of preparation seems, even from a military point of view, stupid. We have everything to lose and nothing to gain through chemical-biological destruction. By our leadership we show the way to small nations who might have everything to gain and little to lose by attacking us with such weapons. They could even blame us for starting the process. Their fear of us might be their excuse.

Until 1974 we refused to sign the Geneva protocol that bans the use of such weapons; sixty-two other nations had signed it. Of the large nations, only the United States and Japan had refused. Our policy was that we would reserve the right to do as we want.

The Senate ratified the 1925 Geneva Protocol banning the use of chemical and bacteriological weapons in December of 1974. President Ford signed the treaty on January 22, 1975. But the document does not solve the problem. Tear gas and herbicides are still allowed under certain conditions. There is no machinery for verification, in order to be sure that those signing the treaty are honoring it. The issue of controlling stockpiles and production of lethal chemicals still continues. In 1975 a new training program in the use of nerve and mustard gas got underway at Redstone Arsenal, using live chemicals.

In 1959, Congress opposed Robert W. Kastenmeier's resolution which stated, "The United States shall under no circumstances resort to the use of poisonous or obnoxious gases unless they are first used by our enemies." The State Department, the Pentagon, and the American chemical companies opposed the resolution.

President Nixon's declaration in November, 1969, that the United States would not be the first to use chemical agents and that the United States would destroy its stockpile of biological weapons and would not use them is a step in the right direction. This was brought on partly through the intense efforts of Representative Richard

McCarthy and the attention the news media paid to these horror agents. It illustrates how publicity about what we are doing can force a change.

The fact that United States was faced with a U.N. General Assembly resolution renouncing the use of these weapons helped Mr. Nixon make the decision.

But it is an incomplete step. It still allows the use of gas and chemical defoliants, which, in the opinion of many, violates the Geneva agreements. It still allows research on the production of biological weapons. It states that in practice we have always followed the Geneva agreements. This is doubtful. Many consider our use of gas and defoliants in Vietnam a violation of these agreements. It is also interesting to note the lack of symmetry in our unilateral renunciation of biological weapons and our demand for bilateral policy in nuclear weapons.

Morally there is no argument for the use of chemical-biological death agents. They are offensive weapons which cannot be controlled so that they do not strike the innocent. They open a Pandora's box of all kinds of horror weapons. The lame military excuse that we need to reply in kind[16] would make just as much sense as saying that since the Soviets use the philosophy of Communism against us, we should teach our soldiers the philosophy of Communism so that they could reply in kind.

Harvard biologist Dr. Matthew Meselson thinks that these weapons do not add to the over-all security of this nation. Rather, because they are fundamentally directed against people, against wide areas, they are useful only in surprise attack. "They are terror weapons; they are panic weapons."[17]

Why are we interested in CBW? Are we interested in making war cheaper so poorer nations can join the "big" games? Are we interested in surprise attack? Are we interested in destroying civilian populations? When a girl in my class learned that the army was developing a "continuous-paste machine" for producing germs, she asked: "If eight ounces is enough to kill all the world, why is the army interested in such a machine?" There are no good answers. Seymour Hersh says, "You just don't understand the military mind when you ask a question like that. They are not interested in meeting a need. They just want to go as far as they can."[18] It is probably the inability to give a good answer that induces the army to surround CBW research and deployment with extensive secrecy.

The Federation of American Scientists believes that the development, testing, and deployments by the United States of biological and chemical weapons of mass destruction is pointless, dangerous, and provocative and should be discontinued. They cannot see how our national security is promoted. They see the weapons as a danger to us, both from accidents and by encouraging smaller nations to develop them.[19]

This statement reflects the worry of many scientists about the use of science for destruction. Many of them feel that the engineers and scientists who cooperated with Hitler in the development of the ovens and gases for concentration camps are not innocent of guilt. The scientists cannot, with good conscience, say that the work is neutral, that the decisions to kill are made by the government. A person cannot say this if he or she is working on a weapon. The person is a necessary instrument for that government, necessary to effect the killing.

We all have a responsibility for what our government does, especially in a democracy. In preparation for chemical-biological war, we have a good clear issue on which to take our stand. The conscience of man opposes it. Even the military are ashamed of it and say they never really intend to use it.

If the populace can close its eyes to this possible crime against humanity, we have no hope. The devastation through these weapons is more horrible and potentially more widespread than nuclear war itself.

Chapter 2

THE EXAMPLE OF CHRIST AND TODAY'S CONVENTIONAL WISDOM

Lunching at the University of Minnesota, another priest and I were discussing the just-war theory and how it applied to Vietnam. Between us a University of Minnesota student sat pensively. After a while, he said, "When I listen to a couple of clergymen like you, I am glad I am an atheist. Both of you agree that the Vietnam war is wrong, but you go through a long lot of talk and argument that I can't see any need for. Why not just say that the war is inhuman?"

The student had a good point. If the Christian Gospel were so complex on an issue as clear as killing in war, then who would be able to understand the Gospel? Who would be able to live by it?

Does the Christian Gospel give approval to war? If not, how do Christians get into the position of accepting both the Gospel and war?

It is not a question of ability to use force or approval of the establishment of order. Force is used in police action, but police action is not killing in war. Police action is different than war action. Police ordinarily do not try to kill

29

but to arrest. Police usually are limited to their own
territory and work under the framework of their country's
laws. They do not ordinarily attack groups or use weapons
of massive destruction. A police force can develop to
resemble the military especially in time of war. Generally
police are different enough from the military that you can
separate them both physically and morally.

War is intergroup lethal conflict. Historically it has
these characteristics: a) much killing b) spiritual and
psychological mobilization of group against group c) a
momentum of its own which results in savagery unplanned
by either side.

It is especially the taking of human life and the
mobilization of group hatred that puts the question into
focus. Does the Christian Gospel ever approve of war, or
does it teach a special way of meeting evil and suffering?
Is this Christian way of meeting suffering so destroyed by
war that the Christian can never approve of war?

Clearly the Gospel does not give approval to war. The
Christian Gospel has a core message summarized by Jesus
himself: "Love one another." This is part of Jesus' basic
teaching that all men and women are brothers and sisters,
children of the same God, and that because of this all have
an almost infinite value.

The law of love includes all people not only our own
families or our own country. "Love your enemy" clearly
makes it universal. To have the Gospel approve of war we
would have to read it as meaning that we can love our
enemies by killing them.

The whole attitude of the Gospel is far from this.
"Return not evil for evil, but good for evil." "Blessed are
they that suffer persecution." The Gospel is an invitation
to love God and our neighbor; it is an appeal to the heart
and to the truth. War is opposed to this. War is forcing
others through fear and death to accept the demands
made.

The Christian faith teaches that the doubt is to be resolved by looking at the example of Jesus. He is the incarnate embodiment of what the Christian teaching says; his life, and especially his death, should explain anything that is doubtful in the message of love and peace.

Viewed in this manner, it is perfectly clear that the massive killing that goes on in war has no support from the Gospel.

How then does the Christian clergyman get into such a strange position of mouthing long theories? It wasn't that way in the beginning. During the first three centuries the constant teaching of all the Fathers of the Church was that baptism into Christ forbade Christian participation in war. Not a single Father of the Church in those centuries approved of Christian participation in war.[1]

Only after Emperor Constantine became a Christian in 312 A.D. did Christians begin to change. They discovered a way of embracing both war and the Gospel. They did this by the "just-war theory," first developed by St. Augustine in the fourth century. It says that under certain strictly-adhered-to conditions, a particular war might be an exception to the Gospel and not a violation of it. In fact, with these conditions fulfilled, Augustine argued, war would be an act of love and mercy.

The theory is a relatively simple one, with several conditions:

1. War is permissible only after all other efforts have failed.

2. The intention of the war must be good—for example, defense against attack.

3. Non-combatant immunity must be preserved—no burning, massacre, or killing of the innocent.

4. The force used in war should be proportionate to the goals sought.

These conditions must be applied every day of the war. If the conditions in the war change, or the intention changes, then a completely different moral situation exists. The theory also says that any essential defect of any of these conditions at any time would make any war wrong, making it a violation of the Gospel and not an exception.

I was discussing these points with my fellow clergyman in Minnesota when the young student made his observation. His comments brought to mind the weaknesses of the just-war theory.

WEAKNESSES OF THE JUST-WAR THEORY

1. The theory never worked in practice. From the time it was first conceived to the present, there is no record of any nation's ever using it. No nation today accepts it as national policy. Even after wars were over, no conference of bishops ever condemned any war on the basis of this theory—neither their own war nor the war of any other nation.[2]

2. The theory presupposes the very thing it is supposed to prove: that some killing is allowed on human authority.

3. It assumes that in war one side will be just and the other unjust; this never happens. Instead both sides, for example, the Germans and Americans kill each other in God's name and both claim they are right.

4. The theory was formulated to show that *some* wars might be an exception to the law of the Gospel; it has become a theory used to justify every war that comes along. Instead of justifying an exceptional war, it is used to make all war acceptable.

5. It allows each nation to judge its own cause. This violates the common-sense adage that no one is an unbiased judge of his own cause.

6. It requires a truthful presentation of all the issues and facts before and during the war. Does any nation

today tell the truth about its war intentions or operations? Does the army tell you what it is planning to do so that you can make a judgment about it? Those who manned the American bombers that attacked the city of Dresden in Germany were not told they were bombing a city. They were told lies; they thought they were attacking military targets. How many lies are told in wars?

7. How could you ever know enough of the intent and action of nations and governments to make a sure judgment? Yet, according to Christian morality, you must be certain of your decision before you can excuse killing. This theory would mean that an 18-year-old American must decide on an urgent issue in favor of life or death. As the Minnesota student says, of what use is it if the Gospel and the theory need all this interpretation and weighing of hidden facts?

8. The just-war theory is essentially a "limited-war" theory. Total war and nuclear technology have no relation to it.

One or another of these weaknesses would be serious. Together they help us to see why this theory is unrealistic and is today outmoded.

The just-war theory is the only attempt at a moral justification of war by Christians. It is the only attempt to relate war to the Gospel. If this is rejected, then the Christian is left with the Gospel, which rejects killing as immoral.

Today, there is an even more pressing need for re-evaluation. One of its weaknesses, the irrelevance of the theory to the nuclear age, is a reason why Pope John called Vatican Council II. He saw the technological development of the world as a process that was by-passing the Church. He called for a streamlining of the Church, and for a re-evaluation of the Church in a modern age in order to make the Church relevant.

Just as the development of the long-range cannon

marked the end of safety for the walled castle, so the
development of modern nuclear technology rendered the
just-war theory obsolete. Pope John recognized this in his
encyclical *Peace on Earth*.

The Pope looked on the world from the perspective of
his own experience and his heart, which was open to all
that was human, and from his position as the father of the
human family. The solidarity of the human family was the
essence of his vision. To justify war in any form, Pope
John would have had to deny this family unity—war would
demand a division of man into the just and the unjust.

Pope John put forth the new perspective on war and
peace which the Vatican Council reflected in its decisions.
He suggested the Gospel of non-violence. He said,
"There can be no doubt that relations between states, as
between individuals, should be regulated not by the force
of arms but by the light of reason, by the rule, that is, of
truth, of justice and of active and sincere cooperation."

Pope John's faith in non-violence is a faith in the human
spirit's permanent capacity to open itself to truth. He saw
the failure of Christians to trust in the truth of faith and
their willingness to resort to the use of force as a failure of
faith. Pope John declared that peace is to be found not in
"equality of arms, but in mutual trust alone." He saw
trust as the way to peace, and fear as the road to war. He
said, "In every human being, there is a need that is
congenital to his nature, and that never becomes
extinguished, compelling him (man) to break through the
web of error and open his mind to the knowledge of
truth."[4] He extended this desire, this need for truth, to
every man no matter how bad he might be. There is
always hope that man's need for truth will lead him out of
his error. As Pope John said: "God will never fail to act on
his interior being with the result that a person who at a
given moment of his life lacks the clarity of faith . . . can
at a future date be enlightened and believe in the truth."

This means that not even a Hitler is beyond hope.

In this kind of view Pope John was in thorough agreement with Gandhi, who said, "Truth is God." Gandhi preferred that statement to "God is Truth." Pope John said that the power of truth is the power of God, not the sword. Thus the conclusion of both Gandhi and Pope John is that non-violence should be the program for every sector of human activity.

Pope John's theology called for no nuclear deterrents for a world-wide community of men. The Council fathers were unable entirely to share John's vision, but his vision was put before them and they responded in some measure.

In the *Constitution on the Church in the Modern World* (par. 80), Vatican II presents a new perspective on war. At the beginning of the statement, it calls for "an evaluation of war with an entirely new attitude" because of the almost total slaughter which threatens mankind from the new weapons.

Article 77 sets the frame of reference for the discussion with the subtitle "The Human Family's Hour of Crisis." Chapter V, Part II, carries the title "The Fostering of Peace and the Promoting of a Community of Nations." These two elements, the solidarity of the human family and the thermonuclear danger, make up the context for the entire discussion of war. They are essential parts of Pope John's vision.

The Council summarizes the attitude in these three elements: a condemnation of area destruction, an appeal to conscience that calls on men in the armed services not to obey blindly but to weigh the morality of the orders they follow, and the praise of non-violence as a specific way of following the Gospel.

With regard to area destruction, the Council says:

Any act of war aimed indiscriminately at the destruction of entire cities or extensive areas along with their population is a crime against God and man himself. It merits unequivocal and unhesitating condemnation [par. 80].

In its entire text, this is the only time that the word *condemnation* is used. Because of the use of this word and the importance of the statement, this passage in a sense becomes the central declaration of the entire Council.

With this statement the Council moves the Church away from the acceptance of the just-war theory. There is no reference here to the weighing of conditions. What this statement says is that the moral limits of war are by-passed when thermonuclear destruction or area destruction is in question. The shift from the just-war framework back to the Gospel of peace of the first three Christian centuries has become a fact. Discussion of this statement in the Council proceedings by Bishop Taylor of Sweden makes the new position most emphatic. Bishop Taylor offered the following statement as an amendment:

As total war is now a war against God's plan, against mankind itself, the actuation of the spirit of Christ is more imperative than ever. Christians should cultivate a deep awareness that violence is an actual expression of hatred and should undertake a fuller exploration of the non-violent love, the teaching of Christ.[6]

The second element that the Council introduced in the new vision on war is conscience. The Council praised conscience with these words: "Actions which deliberately conflict with these same principles [natural law] as well as orders commanding such actions are criminal, and blind obedience cannot excuse those who yield to them" (par. 79).

In Nuremberg, the tribunal said that officers who followed orders are responsible for their actions. They cannot shift responsibility for immoral actions to those who ordered the actions. The United States accepted this idea in the treaty at London.

The final element in the new perspective on peace offered by the Council is a turn to non-violence. The Council said, "We cannot fail to praise those who renounce the use of violence in the vindication of their rights and who resort to methods of defense which are otherwise available to the weaker parties too" (par. 78).

These three elements of a new perspective toward peace are not part of a just-war theory. They clearly and positively point out the path toward peace. It is not a precise and specific path, but it does indicate the way. The new ways initiate a return to the Gospel of love and peace, the Gospel depicts Christ as a lamb and not as a wolf, and the spirit of God as a dove and not an eagle. It brings back the Gospel story which speaks of Christ as a Prince of Peace, not a soldier at arms.

This is the spirit reflected by Vatican II. Instead of trying to show that under certain conditions some war might be just, it makes clear that certain acts of war are wrong. It points out the Christian mission of peace and emphasizes that the Christian Gospel is opposed to all war.

Not long ago a Catholic priest asked me, "Why are they concentrating on calling this war immoral? [Vietnam] What about all other wars?" While this question was asked as a means of evading the discussion of the moral issue of Vietnam, it does bring up the question which should have been asked and answered long ago: Is any war moral?

The failure of the Christian Churches to answer this question clearly is great. In the age of thermonuclear danger that failure is more serious and more evident. The answer is coming now. All forms of contemporary warfare are beginning to be regarded as morally doubtful by Christian leaders. Pope John, Pope Paul, the Vatican Council, and numerous Christian leaders and theologians reflect this trend.

In a recent address to a meeting of the Dutch military chaplaincy, Cardinal Alfrink took the position that a just war is no longer possible, holding that: "The existence of nuclear weapons excludes the existence of a just war because the means that could be used to fight injustice would cause much greater injustices.[7]

Cardinal Lercaro of Bologna dismissed the idea of just war as something "left over from the cases and mental attitudes which no longer have anything to do with the facts."

The same idea is expressed by Bishop Giuseppe Marafini, President of the Italian Bishops' Ecumenical Secretariat. At the August 1969 meeting he declared, "For the church any war is an inhuman, anti-evangelical, and an inadequate means for solving differences."[8] He said the teaching of Pope John, Vatican II, and Pope Paul illustrates the change in the Church's attitude toward war. It is a movement away from the acceptance of any war toward a rediscovery of the Gospel message of peace. It is clear that the Council brought down the curtain on the just-war theory.

The theory was much talked about by theologians, but it had never received any formal theoretical approval from any council of the Church. At Vatican Council II, some bishops tried to have the just-war theory acknowledged and accepted. This was never done. No formal reference to the theory was ever made, not even in a footnote.

The Council, working within the context of the massive power of new weapons and the solidarity of the human family, called for a new evaluation of war. It is in this context that two statements of the Council should be understood. One statement says:

As long as the danger of war remains and there is no competent and sufficiently powerful authority at the international level, government cannot be denied the right to legitimate defense once every means of peaceful settlement has been exhausted [par. 78].

The other statement is:

Those too who devote themselves to the military service of their country should regard themselves as the agents of security and freedom of peoples. As long as they fulfill this role properly, they are making a genuine contribution to the establishment of peace [par.79].

Taken in their context, these two statements put in doubt the question whether any war today can be legitimate. The first statement speaks of "legitimate defense, after every peaceful means has been exhausted." This does not say it is ever "legitimate" for a Christian to get involved in the mass killing of war.

In its explicit condemnation of area destruction and its call to conscience and the praise of non-violence, the Council itself makes very clear that certain types of war are illegitimate. A war that by-passes the international organization which is the last, best hope of peace, the United Nations, is never legitimate.

The second statement with the limitation "as long as they fulfill this role properly" leaves open the question whether this role could ever be properly fulfilled if those in the military service are engaged in killing.

While war is not entirely condemned, mass killing is never condoned. The new statements show where war must be condemned in contrast to the just-war theory, which sought to give conditions under which war may be waged. Notice that in neither of these two statements does the word *war* appear. Neither of these statements from Vatican Council II says that war, as we have it today, is just under certain circumstances. At the most these statements show that Pope John's vision of peace was not fully shared by the Council; however, even these statements, which were the best that the proponents of the just-war theory could get in the Council, do not support the just-war theory. That has been clearly discredited by the call for a new evaluation along lines proposed by the Council.

The context of Vatican II casts strong doubt on whether any war could be legitimate today. That doubt arises from the fact that nuclear war is certainly condemned and that conventional war today comes under the same condemnation because it involves the intent or threat to use nuclear weapons. Since it is immoral to use these area-destruction agents, it also is wrong to intend to use them; therefore, a war which might depend on this background threat is immoral because it involves an evil intent. [9]

This is the position taken by a native Bishop of Puerto Rico, Bishop Antulio Parrilla-Bonilla. Speaking before the students of the University of Puerto Rico on April 23, 1969, he condemned any use of nuclear arms as "immoral and criminal." He went on to say: "International war today is immoral because of the risk of releasing a universal suicide." It is also immoral, he said, because it by-passes an international organization already in existence which would be capable of acting as police and repressing the aggressive nation. [10]

Bishop Parilla-Bonilla's statement expresses just what Vatican II has said, namely that in a thermonuclear age any kind of war unreasonably threatens nuclear war. If we describe nuclear war as a war in which entire population centers or even entire populations may be destroyed by the blast, fire storm, burns, or the mutation of hereditary cells by radiation, then it seems that, in the light of the statements of Vatican II, such a war is never justified—even as a defensive war.

Historically the word *war* has these characteristics: much killing, psychological mobilization of group hatred, and a momentum that results in much unplanned savagery. Nuclear war with these characteristics quite clearly could never be moral.

Bishop Parilla-Bonilla's second argument is that any war today should be judged immoral if it unreasonably weakens the United Nations or any world peace instrument of the future. Such weakening actions would violate the obligations set forth in Vatican II: "It is our clear duty to strain every muscle in working for the time when all war can be completely outlawed by international consent. This goal undoubtedly requires the establishment of some universal public authority acknowledged as such by all."[11]

President Kennedy called the United Nations "our last hope in an age where the instruments of war have far out-paced the instruments of peace." Pope Paul in his speech to the United Nations, October 4, 1965, said to the UN Assembly; "You are a bridge between peoples. You are a network of relations between states . . . in the ideological construction of mankind, there is, on the national level, nothing superior to this. Your vocation is to make brothers not only of some, but of all peoples."[12] In view of these and other statements, there is no doubt that the United Nations is the prime candidate for development as an instrument of peace, and it follows that any actions unreasonably weakening the United Nations are therefore wrong and immoral.

In brief, we have developed our weapon power to such a point that it no longer protects us. Never have we had more powerful weapons and never have we been less secure. We have already passed the stage where more power in weapons will bring any advantage. Rather, we have been forced by the power of our weapons to start considering what should have guided us in the first place: respect for human life, self-survival, and the survival of others.

Likewise, the word has developed national power to a degree that no longer shields but now endangers us. National power could destroy both our ideals of freedom at home and peace in the world. We have reached a point in history where no nation alone can defend itself, where international cooperation, which should have been our goal, is now our only political hope.

We have been forced by the circumstances of weapon power and national power to consider the moral values which always should have been our guide. We can now see plainly that compounding violence is in no way a useful response.

For the first time in history, we consider the wisdom of the Gospel: "Do not be overcome by evil, but overcome evil with good" (Romans 12:21). "Love your enemy"—not because we have reached some new level of moral development, but because we see that without principles like these we have nothing to guide us and to save us from destruction.

We are experiencing the force of which Pierre Teilhard de Chardin spoke, the technological progress of man which is forcing us to unity, forcing a convergence of man with other men; in other words, facing men with the alternative of cooperating with each other or destroying each other.

THE DRAFT

One point at which the theory of peace enters into the practical political life of today is in the refusal to go to war because of conscience. A sign of the change isVatican II's statement: "It seems right that laws make humane provisions for the case of those who for reasons of conscience refuse to bear arms." [13]

In the United States this was followed by the American bishops' 1968 declaration and their call for the Selective Service System to open itself to the conscience of those who object to particular wars. This marks the first time that the Catholic Church has gone on record officially in favor of conscientious objection to war, either on the international level or on the American national scene. For that reason, it is worth reviewing the Selective Service System in the United States. A close look at the draft shows that it is both unconstitutional and immoral.

General Hershey liked to look on the Selective Service System as being as American as apple pie. He said on television that the registrant for the Selective Service has no rights except the right to be conscripted.

I was present at a group interview with General Hershey where a young man asked him whether it were true that the first peacetime conscription law passed in the United States was in 1948. He and his assistant, Colonel Omer, replied by talking about conscription in the colonial army, citing vague stories of one hundred years ago. These two men refused to admit even under repeated and earnest questioning that the first peacetime conscription truly was in 1948.

But the history of the United States shows that we came as immigrants escaping the wars of Europe. When we wrote our Constitution, we had a strong determination that we would not accept the quartering of armies among our people or the conscription laws from which we had escaped. The Constitution itself says nothing that can justify conscription. It is doubtful, from the Constitution, whether the federal government has the right to raise an army. This was the view expressed in all the discussions of Congress from 1790, when George Washington first suggested conscription, until the CIVIL War. A typical example of the expressions of Senators and Congressman was given by Congressman Daniel Webster:

Where is it written in the Constitution, in what article or section is it contained that you may take children from their parents and parents from their children, and compel them to fight the battle of any war in which the folly or wickedness of the government may engage itself . . .?

Who will show me any Constitutional injunction which makes it the duty of the American people to surrender everything valuable in life, and even life itself, whenever the purposes of an ambitious and mischievous government may require it . . .?

. . . A free government with an uncontrolled power of military conscription is the most ridiculous and abominable contradiction and nonsense that ever entered into the head of man.[14]

Congress said "no" to the requests for a conscription law up to the time of the Civil War, when the first limited draft law was adopted by the federal government. It was promptly declared unconstitutional by the Supreme Court of Pennsylvania. This decision was overturned, and the right to conscript has been upheld by the Supreme Court in many cases.

During both World Wars, the military made efforts to obtain universal military conscription, which would consolidate the power they gained during war. During World War I, conscription met with significant Congressional opposition. In the April 1917 debate, Rep. George Huddleston from Alabama said, "Conscription is state slavery. It is involuntary servitude, not for crime."[15]

Congressman Carl Hayden from Arizona said:

Much as I dislike to believe it, yet I am convinced that most of the propaganda in favor of selective conscription is founded not so much upon a desire to win the war as it is to accustom the people to this method of raising armies and thereby to establish it as a permanent system in this country.[16]

A Selective Service Law was adopted and signed by Woodrow Wilson on May 18, 1917. This was a wartime law authorizing the draft of all male citizens between their 21st and 31st birthdays. Ministers, divinity students, and certain public officials were exempted.

During the war, in 1918, a push was made by the military to impose universal military training that would not be subject to periodic congressional review. The push failed when brought to a vote in the Senate in 1918. Another effort made after the war was again opposed, and a system of volunteer recruitment was adopted with the national Defense Act of 1920. General Douglas MacArthur endorsed this act and said, "Tradition and public sentiment have always precluded the conscription as the basis of a peace time defense policy." [17]

As the threat of World War II faced America, the military again pushed for Selective Service legislation in September 1940. Opposition was very strong in Congress. Rep. Jerry Voorhis of California said:

I believe that what we are asked to vote on in this bill . . . [is] the adoption of compulsory selective military training and service as a permanent policy for the United States of America and to do it under the impulsion of an "emergency." . . .

It is going to be difficult ever to repeal such a measure once you get it established, for you will have made of your military establishment one of the greatest economic factors in your whole country. You will have vested the greatest power in the Executive and the Army that the Congress has ever granted in all American history.[18]

Senator James Frazier of Tennessee argued, "pass this [conscription bill] . . . and we will have forged the first link in the chain which will drag down America to the same militaristic level of communistic Russia, Fascist Italy and Nazi Germany." [19]

The 1940 act was adopted for one year only. It was the first peacetime conscription for the United States. It was extended in 1941 by a one-vote margin in the House, 203 to 202.

During 1944 the military again maneuvered to impose universal military training as a permanent pattern on American society. Selective Service legislation was not renewed immediately after World War II. A strong coalition helped defeat it and the draft law expired on March 31, 1947. But after the Czechoslovakian coup, a crisis thought by some to have been exaggerated by the army into a false war-scare, conscription was reinstated at the appeal of President Truman in 1948. It has survived up to the present and recently has been amended, in 1967 and 1969.

In all of the debates on peacetime conscription, two main arguments were used against it: the undemocratic and compulsory nature of a system that amounted to servitude and the power it gave the President to engage in overseas military adventures without consulting Congress. Without conscription, it would have been quite impossible for President Johnson to build up the Vietnam war forces to 550,000 men. He would have had to go to Congress for approval of the draft before he acted.

The present Selective Service System rests basically on local boards (4,092 at the peak of the Vietnam War). It is a combination of congressional legislation, of presidential orders, and of housekeeping directives by the director of the Selective Service.

The congressional legislation calls for the registration of all males from 18 to 26 years of age. It exempts ministers, medical students, dentists, and a few others. It allows great executive powers to the President. It exempts him, for example, from the Administrative Procedure Act, which requires the Executive to follow certain steps when he lays out directives having the force of law. For example, the Administrative Procedure Act in reference to the preparation of meat, the slaughtering of pigs, and the selling of almost all consumer products contains provisions guarded by legal procedures protecting the consumer. But none of that has to be gone through in the Selective Service Law. The President is free to set up the procedure simply by decree.

Far worse were the directives of General Hershey.

According to the law, he was limited to housekeeping direction, through memoranda to local boards and letters to the legislative representatives or state directors; although none of these directives have the force of law, they are followed by most of the local boards. Since they are not law, there is no record of them—in fact, until 1969 even when you or a lawyer requested a copy of the directives, it could not be obtained. For example, the Selective Service director sent a letter to the local board suggesting that those who turned in their draft cards be classified as delinquents and as 1A. He could argue that this was merely a directive that the Selective Service Boards did not have to follow. When, in fact, they did follow it, they could say that they were following their own discretion. Because of the vagueness of the law, it is very difficult to seek judicial remedy from the injustices arising from the boards' own actions and interpretations.

Let me try to clarify this point. If a registrant feels that he has been unjustly classified—perhaps denied conscientious objector status—he must commit a felony by refusing induction before he can bring his case to court.

In other situations where any injustice is threatened or damage is imminent, an injunction can be obtained to block that damage. For example, if I work in a federal agency and this agency refused to allow me to make a speech to a certain group, I may go to the courts and bring an injunction restraining the head of this agency from blocking my speech. With the Selective Service Board, however, I must violate the orders and get arrested before I can get the courts to adjudge the merits of my case.

Until the Seeger decision of the Supreme Court in 1965, applicants for conscientious objector status had a special advantage if they belonged to a "peace church" like the Quakers. The Seeger decision ruled out "belief in a relation to a Supreme Being" as a requirement for classification as a conscientious objector.[20] In 1967

Congress took out the requirement of "belief in a Supreme Being" and left only a requirement of "religious training and belief". The Welsh decision of June 15, 1970 gave a broad meaning to the word religious. "Religious" was interpreted to mean "deeply and sincerely held beliefs which are purely ethical or moral in source and content" ... "Because his beliefs function as a religion in his life" such an individual is as much entitled to "religious conscientious objector status" . . . as is someone who derives his conscientious opposition to war from "traditional religious convictions".

The Welsh decision was essentially a restatement of the Seeger decision. The local boards responded to the change so slowly that it was 1970 before the Form 150 reflected the change in questions asked that were to be filled out by the conscientious objector. Local boards still retained discretionary power to decide on all applicants. The local board decided on each case. There are no national standards whose proven fulfillment entitles any citizen to exemption. The standards deal with eligibility to apply for exemption. They give no right to exemption.

Another aspect that is of doubtful constitutional validity is that the law allows a local board to deny the registrant presence of counsel or of a witness when he makes his personal appearance. This is a denial of due process because a juridical judgment that may mean life or death is being made about the registrant.

The operation of the system has been criticized as unfair by many political leaders. One reason is the isolated and often arbitrary decisions of 4,092 different draft boards. During the Vietnam War these boards had members who were characteristically about 58 years old, former members of the American Legion, white, and largely opposed to the idea of conscientious objection.

The law is bad from a legal and constitutional point of view. It is vaguely framed: It allows much discretionary power to the local boards, who are generally unprepared by their background or their training to make such decisions; it creates such disrespect for law in the minds of the young and other thinking citizens that it would be far better for the United States, even from a political point of view, that this law should end. The draft destroys freedom, even for those who are not sent into the service; it destroys an individual's opportunity to choose his own future.

The draft divides the country; it exploits the poor and the talents of all young men, especially the least powerful politically and economically. During the Vietnam War the draft forced an estimated 85,000 young men into political exile and imprisonment, or desertion. Two hundred thousand violations of the Selective Service Law were reported to the Justice Department, unknown tens of thousands did not register; 8,000 were convicted of violations.

The draft destroys our values. It departs from the American tradition which has always regarded conscription as alien to the American way of life; it undermines the ideal of voluntary service given to one's community and nation; it violates conscience. Because of the peacetime draft that has been with us since 1968, we easily forget that in all our previous history we had only 11 years of draft during the civil war and the two world wars. We forget that many immigrants came here to avoid the demands of the standing armies of Europe. For those who were born since 1945, the age of the nuclear weapon, and the age of the peacetime draft starting in 1948, there's nothing to forget. They never knew anything. You have to be older, to be over 30, to remember an America that didn't have the peacetime draft. This is a big change in America, one that was pictured as the destruction of the republic in the days that the draft was argued. We even forget that in 1977 the selective service system is still in force, although no one is being drafted at the present time. The system to start the draft at any time is still there.

The draft has militarized our nation. It adds greatly to the influence of the military establishment in our country by giving it power to control involuntary servitude. Under the pretense of producing a citizen army, it simply gives more status to our professional army. Through military indoctrination and brainwashing and training in the use of weapons, conscription contributes substantially to the spread of violence in the United States of today and the United States of tomorrow. The draft is obsolete. It is an inefficient, unfair, expensive, and unnecessary way to provide for national defense.

The draft hurts us internationally. It weakens democratic control over foreign policy and it provides manpower for military intervention overseas without approval by Congress and the people.

The law is immoral because it does not allow sufficient room for conscience. It requires that a man go and kill in a war in which he does not believe, or go to prison.

The law allows him to apply for the status of conscientious objector but requires that he be opposed to "participation in war in any form." Even then it gives him no right to claim conscientious objector status. The law gives the power to decide that point to a local board. The local board has broad discretionary powers and is guided by no national standards.

If the young man is opposed to a particular war, like Vietnam, but not all wars, his appeal is denied. If he is opposed to all wars but the board does not accept his arguments, his appeal is denied. He must then either follow his conscience and go to prison, or violate his conscience by going to war. A law that requires this is immoral. It violates conscience.

Because the law is immoral, there is good reason to

argue, as many do, that it is also immoral to register under such a law and carry a draft card.

Vatican II said that no one is free to evade his personal responsibility by allowing the government to make his moral decisions. This statement supports those who, on moral grounds, oppose the Selective Service System in one way or another.

Chapter 3

CONVENTIONAL WAR TODAY

The point is often made about Vietnam that the war there was not nuclear war: it was "conventional war." In reality, however, it is "conventional" only in the sense that nuclear weapons are not being used. It is unlike any other war, partly because it went through a unique process of evolution.

In this evolution, heroism, courage, and other human qualities, became less decisive in winning the war than the possession of technological superiority caused by the growth of technology itself. The capacity of bigger and better weapons to destroy more and more people was one element of this evolution.

Another element was a lessening of moral restraints in the conduct of the war. The idea of the rules of war accepted in the 19th century (like the idea that one nation would make war only against the military forces of the enemy and not the civilian population) gave way as the presence of the new technology made it possible to strike at the civilian population and gave a new reason for such strikes: civilians were necessary for the support of the war effort.

This evolutionary process is reflected in the percentage of civilians killed from World War I up to the present. In World War I, 5 per cent of those killed were civilians. In World War II, 48 per cent were civilians. In the Korean War, 84 per cent were civilians; and Philip Berrigan may be right when he estimates that more than 90 per cent of the casualties in Vietnam will turn out to be civilians. [1]

The jump ahead in the technology of destruction is most clearly seen in the development of the thermonuclear weapons; but it can also be seen in the evolution of the airplane. In World War I, the airplane arrived on the scene quite late. The war was over before its capacity for destruction was fully utilized; but the airplane was even then the weapon that most dramatically gave the soldier the wings to go over the head of the enemies and to reach the cities behind the front line.

By 1943, the use of the airplane was so developed that several thousand Royal Air Force planes destroyed the city of Hamburg with massive bombing. Some thirty square miles of the city were damaged, and 12 square miles were burned out by the fire storm resulting from the mixture of incendiary and explosive bombs. The number who died was about the same as in Hiroshima as a result of the atom bombing.

This type of bombing did not happen by accident. It was the result of carefully planned strategy requiring a great deal of coordination of all kinds of skills. The success of this destruction prepared the way for the bombing of other cities—Dresden and Tokyo. The escalation of this power to destroy was matched by the de-escalation of moral indignation and protest at the destruction. The acceptance of the saturation bombing of cities prepared the way for moral acceptance of the atom bombing of Hiroshima.

The brutality of technological warfare showed itself in the prison camps of Germany: Auschwitz, Buchenwald, and Dachau. These camps were not run by depraved sadistic policemen but by soldiers who had given themselves totally to the state without any limitation. The world saw in them what monsters politics united with industrial technology made out of war and out of men. War was no longer the opposition of soldier to soldier; armies were employed against peoples and populations.

This is the theme of the book *An End to Glory* by Pierre-Henri Simon.[2] It is the story of a professional French soldier who quit the army at the age of 40 because his experience in the wars in Vietnam and Algeria brought him to believe that war was no longer human. This soldier's grandfather and father before him had been professional soldiers also, but they had some rules for war and some things that were taboo; for example, they would not torture and kill prisoners. These rules were gone. The role of the soldier was different: without honor.

TODAY'S CONVENTIONAL WEAPONS

The planes used in Vietnam were as different from the planes used in World War II as World War II planes were different from World War I planes. In *Airwar Vietnam*[3] Frank Harvey describes the planes. Some fly at supersonic speeds and are armed with cannons, rockets, napalm, and bombs. Many perform specialized tasks, like the air tanker that refuels other planes; the "hercules" that air lifts troops and equipment; the "Jolly Green Giant," a helicopter that works on air rescue. There are planes and cargo ships that fly intercontinental transport halfway around the world.

The "Huey Hog," a helicopter, did not fly at supersonic speeds hurling its rockets from a distance, but rather came down, "muttering death," as it took part in search and destroy missions. These gunships have four fixed 7.62-mm machine guns and two more on flexible mounts, pods of rockets on either side of the door, and a grenade launcher that hurls many 40-mm grenades per minute. "When a Huey Hog lets loose with all its armament," Harvey writes, "you feel as if you were inside an exploding ammo factory." [4]

"Puff, the Magic Dragon," is the name given to the pre-World War II DC-3, equipped with three electronically controlled and automatically aimed "miniguns," which fire at the rate of 600 bullets per minute—10 per second—from each gun. Every fifth bullet is a tracer. During the early missions the stream of tracers was compared to "the fiery breath of a dragon," suggesting the gunship's popular name. [5]

First-line airplanes like the A-6 Intruder, the F105 Thunderchief, and the F-4 Phantom are equipped with electronic "black boxes." These do more than just provide automatic flight control. They contain systems integrating attack and navigation equipment. There is also a ballistics computer, which helps stabilize the aircraft as a flying platform for rocket and missile firing.

All this has made a big difference both in speed and in fire power. In World War II, it was considered a great accomplishment when planes flew from England to bomb Italy. In the Vietnam War, the B-52s left Guam to bomb in North Vietnam, 2,500 miles away. Guided by electronic communication with forward air observers and a small plane near the target, each carried fifty-one 750-pound bombs. The bombs are dropped from 30,000 or 40,000 feet—too high to be seen or heard. Their target is marked for them by electronic devices both on the ground and in the plane below them. The B-52s were twenty years old; but they used new equipment and new weapons to wage a new kind of war. With a rain of firebombs they destroyed fifty square miles of jungle.

The "automated battlefield" was a feature of 1971-1972 as American military were being withdrawn. Tens of thousands of sensors, like darts with wire antenna attached, were dropped over large enemy areas. They picked up vibrations of the ground or of human voices or sounds. Small radio receiver sender sets were dropped near them. Through these sensors information on the location of these vibrations was radioed to a constantly hovering plane aloft. This plane was connected with computers stationed in Thailand. The computer analyzed the input and alerted an attack plane to bomb the area. The attack plane could be computer directed at night or fly without pilot—a drone plane— by day.

Air war was only one aspect of the change. Aircraft carriers and submarines were now nuclear powered. Even if the submarines did not carry nuclear missiles, they would still be capable of more destruction because they could stay under water longer and go farther without refueling.

Rockets and ballistic missiles that can travel around the earth do not have to carry nuclear warheads. They can carry napalm, biolgical agents, or nerve gas. This could still be called "conventional" war. The speed and direction of the weapons, however, even conventional ones, are now guided by satellite communication, which allows army commanders on the other side of the world to join in a part-line discussion with front-line commanders and political leaders. Penetration can be complete and rapid. Speed, both of communication and of delivery, has changed the nature of "conventional" warfare.

One difference between the conventional war of today and of earlier days is not merely the number that can be or are killed but lies in the very quality of the warfare: it is less human. There is more distance between the killer and the killed. An essential part of the training of the soldier always was to develop "distance." The soldier should not see the face of the man he killed—it might prove too much for him to realize that he was murdering another human being; so he is trained to see the other person as a target, an enemy, a number. This type of training was more difficult when the soldier had to be close to the person he was going to kill. Now it is easier because the soldier can kill from a distance.

Technology has put more distance between the killer and his victim in today's conventional war. The man in the war room, safe beneath the earth, who pushes a button to release a ballistic missile, or the bombardier in a B-52 who is 40,000 feet above the earth does not see the face of the man he will kill.

Distance between the killer and victim has lessened the normal inhibition to killing, the inhibition caused by man's recognition of his fellow-man as human, as a brother. The enemy is known only as a danger, an object fashioned by propaganda into a demon.

IDEOLOGICAL WARFARE

In earlier conventional war the enemy was demonized as much as possible. He was the "barbarian," the "Hun," or the "yellow menace"; but even these categories had something more human about them than the stereotypes pictured in the ideological warfare that has become prevalent today. The "Communist" is no longer seen as a person but as an idea promoter. He is looked upon as the opposite of everything that is good: an atheist opposed to private property and capitalism and out for world conquest. This type of propaganda has its counterpart in the acceptance of the destruction of civilian populations, the use of nuclear weapons, and the call for unconditional surrender. In the fight against an ideology, anything is allowed. All moral restraints and limits are put aside. Technology is called in to do its work.

Some sort of absolute must be invoked in order to

provide a base for every argument. Whether it is a historical creation, a nation erected into an idol, a race, or a class it leads to nothing but slavery and brutality. Such an idol allows man to make whatever law suits his technological power.

If the absolute is a spiritual God, then there would have to be some law of God, some sort of resulting order. If the absolute is the "conscience" of man, then somewhere compassion, love, and justice would have a place. However, if the idol is totally man-made, then man may fashion it as he pleases, and the result is a sickness for humanity.

LIMITS IMPOSED ON WAR BY TECHNOLOGY

The jump in the technology of destruction has advanced far ahead of technology of other fields, outpacing man's ability to deal with it. Superficially, there appears to be no limit to what technology can do; however, technology does impose its own limits.

This is illustrated in the war in Vietnam. There we fought a "conventional" war overshadowed by the threat of nuclear war. This may be shown by a question asked of a high State Department official who was lecturing on U.S. nuclear policy. A college student asked, "Why doesn't the United States just tell the North Vietnamese that we will lob a nuclear bomb in on them unless they make peace with us?"

He answered: "The North Vietnamese would just laugh at such a threat; they would know it was a bluff. The North Vietnamese and the Soviets know very well that the United States would not be willing to gamble on a threat like that. The United States, the Soviet Union, and North Vietnam know that a Soviet nuclear missile might be 'lobbed in' on South Vietnam in retaliation. Would the United States get any proportionate advantage out of such an exchange? Would they be willing to take the gamble?" He did not think a clever gambler would risk odds like that.

So, although we have the weapons with which we can destroy, it is not worth the risk. This same risk is present in a policy of conventional escalation. It might bring on the use of nuclear weapons from the other side. Senator Strom Thurmond, who asked for an escalation of the war through a naval blockade or more bombing, received this reply: It is not worth the risk.

"Is it worth the risk of nuclear war?" This question forcefully faces every decision in conventional war today. In this way the presence of nuclear weapons, ready-to-go, limits and changes the mode of conventional war. This is why, I think, no wars have really been settled by victory since the nuclear age began. Korea is still a divided country. France, with superior might, was not able to use that power in Algeria. The United States, the strongest military power in the world, is unable to win in a small non-industrialized nation. Even when a conventional war seems to succeed, for example, the Six-Day War of the Israelis against the Arabs in June 1967, victory is far from complete. Even the October war of 1973 didn't end the conflict. The Arabs are still demanding the return of the land taken. The Israelis are still preparing for more war to retain the territory they captured. Behind the scenes, the nuclear powers talk to each other about what can be done to stop the conflict from becoming nuclear war. The Israeli-Arab conflict presents a scenario which threatens the possibility of nuclear war.

Let us assume that two conditions are required for nuclear war to begin: that a nation possess nuclear weapons and that the circumstances make it worthwhile for a nation to risk using them. Then suppose that at the end of the Six-Day War in which the Arabs were being defeated, President Nasser had had nuclear weapons.

Would he have considered it worth the gamble to save face and destroy Israel? Or, would Israel, in the fight for her existence, deem it worth the risk?

Today, this is not an impossible situation. The Israeli-Arab conflict continues, and Israel has the capacity to make nuclear weapons. Soon the Arabs may also have the use or at least the "protection" of nuclear weapons.

VIETNAM

The Vietnam War illustrates what the threat of nuclear disaster has done to conventional war today. Just as the so-called just-war theory has been outmoded by the new technology, so has the new technology put a limit on what conventional technology can do.

The Vietnam War is like an elephant stomping on a mosquito or a lion swatting a gnat. Senator McGovern has said:

Our deepening involvement in Vietnam represents the most tragic diplomatic and moral failure in our national experience. The mightiest nation in history—a nation with a glorious democratic tradition based on the dignity and brotherhood of man—is with allegedly good motives, devastating an impoverished little state and ravishing the people whose freedom we would protect. In the process we are sacrificing many of our bravest young men, wasting valuable resources and threatening the peace of the world. We are being pulled step by step into a jungle quicksand that may claim our sons and the sons of Asia for years to come. This is the path of which the late General Douglas MacArthur said, "anyone who commits American forces to a land war in Asia ought to have his head examined." [6]

McGovern's statement reflects both the technical evolution of war today and the dehumanizing effects that accompany it.

In order to see more clearly the morality of the Vietnam War we can take up the four conditions stipulated in the outmoded just-war theory previously discussed and apply them to Vietnam. (Why, it may be asked, do I bother with the theory at all when I reject it as a means for justifying war? I do so simply to show that the Vietnam War must be judged immoral even if one seeks to justify it on the basis of this theory.) These humanizing and limiting conditions were:

1. War must be a last resort.
2. The purpose must be good, e.g. self-defense.
3. Non-combatant immunity—no deliberate slaying of innocent citizens.
4. Proportionality—the good must be greater than the evil.

War as a Last Resort

In entering the Vietnam War, the United States violated the United Nations Charter, not once but several times. Chapter 6 of Article 33 of the Charter states: "The parties to any dispute, the continuation of which is likely to endanger the maintenance of international security, shall, first of all, seek a solution by negotiation, inquiry, mediation, conciliation, arbitration, judicial settlement, resort to regional agencies or arrangements, or other peaceful means of their own choice." We did not "first of all" try any of these alternatives which the article says "shall be done."

Article 37 provides: "Should the partners of the dispute of the nature referred to in Article 33 fail to settle it by the means indicated in that article, they shall refer it to the Security Council." We did not do this either.

On January 31, 1966, President Johnson announced that the U.S. was presenting a resolution to the Security Council which would "open the way to the conference

table," and a resolution was placed on the Coun
agenda. On the same day, we resumed our bombing of t
North after a five-week pause. Ten days later, Februa
10, Ambassador Goldberg indicated that the U.S. had
intention of pressing for action on its own Security Coun
resolution. After taking formal steps to put our case befc
the Council, we declined to promote it with our va
economic and diplomatic power. Our long delay put us
flagrant violation of the UN charter and makes it very cle
that we did not use war as "a last resort."

Our Purpose

In his State of the Union Message in 1965, Preside
Johnson explained our presence in Vietnam: "We a
there, first, because a friendly nation has asked us for he
against Communist aggression." At other times ou
leaders have said we were in Vietnam to check Chines
Communist expansion into Southeast Asia or for our ow
security.

The fact is we have constructed a mosaic of purpose
some of them requiring conflicting strategies. This is or
reason why many loyal and intelligent Americans ar
confused about the war. If, for example, we were there t
help a small nation, we had at some point to sto
destroying that nation, its economy, and its ecolog
otherwise, the goal of our presence would certainly b
thwarted. If, on the other hand, we were there to stop th
advance of Chinese communism, it might be necessary t
destroy a small nation in the process.

If our intentions are to be judged from the history of th
Vietnam War and from our actions, then we find mor
conflict. It appears that our actions did not agree with ou
expressed intentions.

In the years 1947-54, the French made a determine
effort to recolonialize Vietnam, a country they had held fo

eighty-five years. During the last four years of that effort to take over South Vietnam, the United States was the main financial and military supporter of the French. It is perfectly clear that during that time the French were not trying to help a small nation but to reconquer it. As supporters of the French, we gave $2.2 billion to help a conquest. We paid 80 per cent of the cost of the war. Certainly, if the French were the aggressors at this time, we shared in the aggression.

How can our intention of helping a small nation be reconciled with the following statements of our President and Secretary of State? On August 4, 1953, President Eisenhower explained our interest in Southeast Asia:

If Indo-China goes, several things happen right away. The peninsula, the last little bit of land hanging on down there, would be scarcely defensible. The tin and tungsten that we so greatly value from that area would cease coming. . . .So when the United States votes 400 million to help that war, we are not voting a give-away program. We are voting for the cheapest way that we can prevent the occurrence of something that would be of most terrible significance to the United States of America, our security, our power and ability to get certain things we need from the riches of the Indo-Chinese territory and from Southeast Asia.

Secretary of State Dulles repeated this argument in March 1954, a month before the Geneva Conference on Indo-China:

It [Vietnam] is an area that is rich in many raw materials such as tin, rubber, oil, iron ore. . . .and in addition to these tremendous economic values, the area has great strategic value. (Southeast Asia is astride the most direct and best developed sea and air routes between the Pacific and South Asia.) It has major naval and air bases. [7]

Were we invited in by a friendly government? When, in

October 1969, Senator Fulbright read the report on the war submitted by General Westmoreland, he found no document in it to show that we had been invited. Since many of our political leaders had claimed we were there by invitation, Senator Fulbright asked the State Department for more information. The reply was that there was no document, but that talks had gone on between the governments and that this was considered the same as an invitation. [8]

Even if we had been formally asked in by Premier Diem, a man whom we had put in the position to ask us, we could hardly argue that this was not self-invitation. The truth is that we barged into a civil war where Vietnamese were fighting Vietnamese. We intervened to change the course of Vietnamese history.

Were we there to contain Chinese influence? If we were our actions do not show it. We set up a series of unpopular military dictatorships n Saigon. We ignored Vietnam's deep-seated antipathy toward China. We assumed that since Ho Chi Minh was a Communist he could not be a nationalist and therefore must be a tool of Peking and/or Moscow.

It is an uncontested fact of history that for a thousand years the people of Southeast Asia, especially the Vietnamese, have vehemently resisted the Chinese. They have shown this resistance in Indonesia, Burma, and India without help from our army. The most powerful moving force in Vietnam, as elsewhere in Asia, is nationalism, not international communism.

Ho Chi Minh, left to his own devices, might have united the Vietnamese as a buffer state against Chinese penetration into Southeast Asia. U.S. policy, far from containing Peking or Moscow, is much more likely to encourage outside Communist power and influence.

The destruction of Vietnamese villages by American bombers, the occupation of city and countryside by

American forces, the spectre of a Western occupation of an Asian country played into the hands of Communist propagandists all over the world. American bombers pounding away on Vietnam have destroyed economic and industrial strength. The resulting chaos was hardly likely to provide a viable government and a barrier to Chinese communism.

Non-Combatant Immunity

Did we take care that the lives of innocent non-combatants are not deliberately killed? This was a guerilla war. It is the very nature of a guerilla war that the guerilla moves among the people as a fish moves in the water. As we made one effort after another to destroy these guerilllas, we slowly targeted our fire power on the peasantry—the people of Vietnam. This is the water in which the fish move.

We bulldozed entire villages, uprooted whole sections of the people, sprayed entire areas with poison; we created more terror among the people of Vietnam, South Vietnam, South and North, than the selective terror inflicted by the National Liberation Front. Over half of South Vietnam's population of some ten million people was forced to move as refugees from 1965-1974. [9]

The dislocations caused by war have shattered the social fabric of Vietnamese life. From a predominantly rural society, today (1975) over 65% of the South Vietnamese population lives in urbanized areas. From an agricultural surplus area, it has become an agricultural deficit area. [10]

It has been seductively easy for us to escalate our fire power until we have dropped 15,197,726 tons of air, ground, and sea munitions in the Indo China war up to '73.[11] (Compare this with 2,000,000 tons of bombs dropped by the United States on two continents in all of World War II. It was easy to concentrate on what we knew best:

bombing from the air, fire power, technology. But this wa
empty progress because, by escalation of fire power, w
lost the allegiance of the people. In a guerilla war, th
winner is the side with the allegiance of the people.

A government that attacks a village from the air or wit
heavy artillery abandons all pretense of protecting th
people of the village. As general Edward G. Landsda
said, "Civilian hatred of the military resulting from suc
actions is a powerful motive for joining the Vietcong."[12]

Both the political strength among the people and th
political weakness of the government we supporte
argued that we targeted our fire power at the people. Th
1968 TET offensive in sixty cities showed how strong th
will of the people was to resist us after all our escalation.
was this offensive that convinced Senator Robert Kenne
that the war could not be won because we were backing
government without supporters.

He pointed out that all our claims of progress in the wa
of the strength of the government we were supportin
and of enemy weakness were proved false by the TE
offensive. He said, "Half a million American soldiers wi
700,000 Vietnamese allies, with total command of the a
total command of the sea, backed by huge resources ar
the most modern weapons, are unable to secure even
single city from the attacks of an enemy whose tot
strength is about 250,000."[13]

Senator Kennedy concluded that this happened becau
we sought to resolve by military might a conflict in whi
the issues depend on the will and conviction of the Sou
Vietnamese people. He said it was like sending a lion
halt an epidemic of jungle rot.

Another evidence that we were not protecting t
innocent sufficiently is the estimate done by the staff
Senator Edward Kennedy as Chairman of the Sen
Committee on Refugees. His staff extensively studied t
casualties inflicted on civilians in Vietnam on both side

The staff estimated that the civilian casualties alone average about 125,000 per year, 430,000 killed; 1,005,000 wounded (total as of Jan. 27, 1974).[14] The bulk of all casualties was due to United States fire power.

Can this number of civilian casualties—to say nothing of military casualties—be used as an argument that we are not sufficiently careful of the lives of the peasants? I think it is very clear that we have violated the non-combatant immunity required for the fulfillment of the just-war theory.

Proportionality

Senator Eugene McCarthy was asked, on a television broadcast, to summarize in thirty seconds why the Vietnam War was immoral. He phrased it this way: If an adult starts beating a child and the child dies, the adult is responsible at some point for the murder. So, when a nation begins to inflict punishment on another nation, if that punishment is out of proportion to the good that might be hoped for, the nation inflicting the punishment becomes guilty of immorality on the principle that its action is doing more harm than good.

This argument means that a proportion is to be kept between the good desired and the evil allowed; good and evil must be weighed. When you apply this principle to Vietnam, we find this result: 58,000 American dead,[15] 338,044 wounded, Vitenamese (north and south) 1,186,180 killed; 1,989,210 wounded, 40,000 South Vietnamese civilians executed without trial under the Phoenix program, over 10 million civilian casualties which is more than half of the 18 million population in South Vietnam. In Laos 300,000 refugees; in Cambodia, 1.4 million refugees out of a population of 7 million. Twenty per cent of South Vietnam forested area (5,205,354 acres) has been sprayed with herbicides and much of it destroyed. Six per cent (562,166 acres) of South Vietnam's cropland has been sprayed extensively and perhaps permanently damaged. During the war we spent over $150 billion on Vietnam while at home the poor and the black have become more angry and frustrated. The gains in civil rights have been slowed by war's savagery.

Abroad we saw our old friends turn from us, more in sorrow than in anger. We waged war almost alone, with few allies; only a few client states were forced by their dependence on us to support our efforts with token help.

What good did we hope for from this war? Officially, we hoped for a negotiated settlement with the participation of a government that is not able to win the allegiance of its people and that is the successor to many previous military dictatorships. When we agreed to the negotiations in 1972 we agreed to what we refused to accept in Geneva in 1954, in 1961, in 1964, and in 1966. Clearly, when you weigh the good we hoped for, against the price that we have paid and are paying, there is no adequate proportion.

In the just-war theory, the war, to be just, would have had to fulfill all four conditions. It is clear to me that the Vietnam War and our participation in it fulfilled none of them. It was an immoral war by every and any moral test. Moreover, in the nuclear age, it can be judged immoral because it unreasonably contributed to the danger of nuclear war and unreasonably by-passed (and therefore weakened) the hope for peace through the United Nations.

More than illustrating the moral failure of the Vietnam War, I think an analysis of its failure to fulfill these conditions also reveals the military failure of the war. It brings up the question of whether or not there is a military test in a nuclear world by which a war, even from military point of view, might be considered a victory. Today perhaps, as Nobel Prize physicist Max Born suggests, "technology and war are incompatible." [16]

Technology has moved war from a battle between

armies to an attack on people. It is no longer a duel but a massacre. If that is the case, technology is forcing us either to reject war altogether as inhuman or to conduct it without moral restraint, according to whatever necessities technology imposes.

Chapter 4

THE PROCESS OF PEACE

"What can I do to promote peace?" This is the question that is often asked as a person becomes concerned about the drift toward disaster. Sometimes it is asked in despair as though the job were so big and impossible that nothing could be done: "What can I, a single person, do against such a large immovable process?"

An example of this involves a friend of mine who was worried about his complicity with the war in Vietnam through his payment in taxes. He kept asking me what he could do to stop the war.

There were many things to do about the war, from informing oneself about the facts to working with Congress to opposing the war. My friend answered that he was already doing these things and still the war continued. I told him it was worth attempting to do the right thing even if we failed.

The hope for the future can be stronger, I believe, if two tangled elements in the situation are separated. One element was simply stopping nuclear war and the arms race.

With regard to stopping war, it is probable that nothing is going to stop it. I say that because of human history and our American history. In the United States we have lived with 400 years of violence. It is a history that tells us to kill Indians, take their property, put them on reservations, and then by film and folklore continue to tell our children that they are savages.

We have a history of 300 years of Negro slavery and another 100 years of segregating the Negro into second-class citizenry. This cultural addiction to violence is part of the reason why more violence is probable.

As Richard Goodwin says in his book *Triumph or Tragedy:*

If a large-scale war ever comes, it will not come in a burst of Strangelove madness or a Fail-Safe accident but through a long series of acts and decisions, each seemingly reasonable, that will slowly place the great powers in a situation in which they will find it impossible to back down. It will be no one's fault . . . but it will be the fault of many—leaders, politicians, journalists, men and women in a hundred different occupations in many lands who failed to see clearly or act wisely, or speak articulately. There will be no act of madness, no single villain on whom to discharge guilt; just the flow of history. [1]

To stop the drift toward war, we have to erase the psychology developed by our long addiction to violence. It is not probable that we can erase this rapidly enough to prevent nuclear war. Many informed and intelligent Americans feel, as I do, that the violence of the Vietnam War moved us closer to the danger of nuclear destruction.

As we think about our nation's history, we should recall the words of Jefferson spoken during the debate on the Constitution after his efforts to have slavery excluded had failed. He said, "I tremble for my country when I reflect that God is just, that His justice cannot sleep forever." [2]

Nations do not repent, so they should expect that they will be punished here in this life. In fact, this is the way that nations are punished: by defeat and downfall, perhaps even destruction. We are now living in the country of Thomas Jefferson. This nation may not be saved from the course of its violent past.

The individual may still do something for the process of peace. In fact, the individual citizen's effort will be all the more needed as public officials fail to act.

The phrase which might guide us is from the Constitution of the United Nations Educational, Scientific, and Cultural Organization (1946): "Since wars begin in the minds of men, it is in the minds of men that the defenses of peace must be constructed."

The greater the danger of war, the greater is the need to reverse the process of war with the process of peace. Everything from individual information and action to organized and international action needs to be done. Individual actions, like the refusal to go into the armed services or the refusal to pay taxes, may not stop the war, but they may start the process of peace.

When Mussolini began to organize his Fascist Party, a notice arrived in a small Sicilian town demanding that all men were to join the Fascist army. That same night, the school teacher posted a notice on the town hall that he would not join, believing that what the Fascists were doing was wrong. As he was being taken out to be shot he was asked, "Why did you place the notice on the Town Hall when you knew it would not do any good?" He answered, "I did not want it to be unanimous." His example remains after the uselessness of fascist violence has become evident.

We can recall, too, that Jesus began with twelve followers to teach his message of peace to the world, to turn people from the belief that violence is the only solution to the differences between people.

Another way of encouraging our interest in peace is to understand that we do not escape the difficulties or the danger in a world which may blow up simply by inaction and apathy toward this danger. Our lives and the witness that we give must help light the way to peace for others. When we work toward peace, we can expect God's help. God's plan is that we should overcome evil with good. And the greatest evil that threatens us today is destruction from the violence of our own hands.

THE WAR PROCESS

We can learn a great deal about the process of peace and its promotion by looking at its opposite, the war process. A war process does not begin with the declaration of hostilities and the explosion of bombs; it is a process growing day after day. It is total and takes in every aspect of life.

We educate toward war. The military toys, soldiers, and guns that we give our children to amuse them, the violence on television, in the cinema, and in the literature and drama of our nation teach violence as a way of life. For more formal education we have four military academies and the national war colleges; we have the peacetime draft system, which channels the lives of the youth of our country into war and violence. We also have the army, navy, marines, and air force ready for war—even before there is a war. The huge bulk of a tax dollar goes for defense spending year after year.

We have a military establishment that can win its aims with its vast budget and powerful political influence. An easy figure to remember is this! Seventy percent (actually 69.8%) of all Federal employees are employed by our Department of Defense and 65 cents of every freely controllable dollar spent from the Presidential budget is

spent for war related expenses. The figure on employee
is easily found in the statistical abstract.[3] The figure o
spending is not generally known or believed.

Presidents present their budgets to the people in such
way that people are led to believe that military spending i
only one third of the budget or less. They use th
category "Defense Budget". They do not refer t
"war-related" expenses. They are correct when they pu
the "Defense Budget" at about 1/3 of the total. The
mislead when they lead the public to believe that this i
the total of war-related expenses.

That total is over 65%. How do you get that figure? Yo
add to the Defense budget expenses for Veterans
expenses for interest on the national debt (90%
war-related), expenses for space technology, and othe
hidden military expenses like the Coast Guard (hidde
under "Commerce and Transportation") and Arm
engineers (hidden under "Natural Resources an
Environment"). Then you subtract from the total budge
the deceptive padding of $136 billion in the Social Securit
Trust Fund. These funds are earmarked exclusively fo
Social Security. The Social Security Trust is an insuranc
scheme, and all salaried workers are required to pay int
it. They collect their benefits after age 65.

The Social Security Fund was considered separately an
not stuffed into the budget until 1968. By taking this out o
the total budget, then comparing all military-related an
military expenses with the total you get 65% of th
controllable budget for military related expenses.

Here is how it worked for 1977:

The total budget for 1977 is about $413 billion dollars
The National Defense Budget is about $112 billion dollars
These figures are somewhat approximate as Congres
changed the figures from the original budget request an
the executive changes the approved expenditures too
spending at a faster or slower rate, depending on circum
stances.

Not included in the National Defense budget are the following war-related expenses: at least $.7 billion in Internal Affairs and Finance, $4.5 billion in Space Research and Technology, $2.2 billion in Natural Resources and Environment, $.8 billion in Commerce and Transportation, (including Coast Guard), $.5 billion in Community Development and Housing, $19.5 billion in Veterans Services and Benefits, $3.8 billion in General Government, and about $36 billion interest on the National Debt. A total of $67.3 billion.

Add this to the $112 billion National Defense budget and you get a total of about $179.3 billion in defense and war-related expenses.

When you subtract the social security stuffing you get:

$ 413 billion	Total Budget
-136 billion	Social Security Payment
$ 277 billion	Total Controllable Budget

Out of a controllable budget of $277 billion dollars, $179.3 billion are war-related, amounting to about 65% of the budget. This $179 billion for war-related expense influences politicans who owe their political careers to supporting defense industries and military spending in their areas. Such politicans are supported by millions of workers in defense plants. Congresspeople or even Presidents who oppose military spending risk losing public support. We now have over 28 million veterans, 23% of the male population! The military machine uses public funds to propagandize the people. Often, the military can effect its will despite the desires of civilian officials. The military even influences the international scene: the United States has treaties to help defend forty-eight nations if they request our aid—or if we intervene.

There are many more subtle influences than the above
Our history books are often stories of our wars, as thoug
there were nothing else to tell. They speak of no mistake
for which we should repent, no enemies who were good
no wars that were bad. They describe heroes characterize
by military bravery. Even public monuments help us t
believe that almost all our heroes were military men. I
history books, usually the atrocities of war and th
killing—which are the central acts of war—are overlooked
In this way our minds, filled with stories of bravery an
endurance, create an image where national pride i
strengthened and the way for more violence is prepared

Many of the best-known army films are made at an arm
center in Long Island, New York. This area was purchase
at a cost of $10 million in 1942. The chief of the Army'
Motion Picture Section points out that "to qualify fo
military cooperation" a film depicting an army subjec
must be a picture that "will reflect favorably on th
Army."[4] Civilian actors in army uniform are highly pai
and are assisted by real soldiers.

The war process works through religious faiths
ministers and priests wear the uniform and receive pa
from the military. Some have high rank in the militar
services. This effectively says to the members of thei
faiths that religion and the army are easily compatible.

The presence of the national flag beside the tabernacl
of worship and of student Reserve Officers Training Corp
on the campuses of prestigious schools says to th
worshiper and to the student that military life is a
religious as God and as normal as going to school.

These subtle indirect influences of the military ove
civilian life are more effective in militarizing society tha
most others. The extent of military penetration int
civilian life is illustrated by the influence of the Reserv
Officers Training Corps (ROTC) once it has becom
established in a school. It is not content with military dril

and lectures. It spreads like an octopus into every facet of an institution.

The ROTC at Georgetown University illustrates this point. ROTC invited the neighboring high school children to come to the Georgetown campus to see captured Communist weapons displayed on the ball field. No doubt the weapons could have been shown at nearby Fort McNair. On the campus of a Christian university, however, they seem not to have been put there by the military, but sanctioned by Christianity.

In these and other ways, the military at an educational institution infiltrates and spreads the philosophy that violence and killing are the American way. This inevitably leads to the conclusion that force and violence, instead of cooperation through some international organization or reconciliation or admission of fault on either or both sides, will solve the world's and the nation's problems.

War is the process that leads to lethal group conflict. Its process is all that divides and separates human beings from each other. such as conflict, oppression, racism, nationalism, fear, hatred, and death. The process of war leads only to death.

Through the war process each generation learns to forget the horror experienced in every war and passes on to the next generation stories of glory and of heroes. Thus, most young people are prepared to shoot when the signal is given.

THE PROCESS OF PEACE

The process of peace is the reverse of the process of war. It is reconciliation between God and my neighbors. It includes all that unites humans with each other and with the divine; co-operation, friendship, marriage, family, racial integration, international unity. It is based on trust, motivated by love, it leads to life. Like the war process it is total, affecting every facet of human thought, action, and organization.

A thorough knowledge of the war process is one of the first tasks in sizing-up the problem of reversing it and turning it toward peace. To help inform oneself on the reality of the present situation of war-ideology domination, books like Sidney Lens, *The Military Industrial Complex*,[5] or one of the others in the brief book list at the end of this book, would be a good start. It is important and not difficult for an ordinary person to gain a basic knowledge of the main themes of these books: nuclear weapons, the economics of war, Vietnam, U.S. foreign policy, and the steps towards peace. Getting this knowledge is a first step towards peacemaking.[6]

Three or four periodicals from the many which cover the activities of the peace process might encourage you to know that you are not alone. Good choices would be: *War-Peace Report*, 300 E. 46th St., N.Y., monthly, single copy 50 cents, subscription $5.00; *Win*, War Resisters League in cooperation with the New York workshop on non-violence, biweekly except during July, August, and December, $5.00 per year; *Fellowship*, Fellowship of Reconciliation, Box 271, Nyack, N.Y., 10960; *The Federalist*, United World Federalists, 1346 Connecticut Ave. NW., Washington, D.C., 20030, monthly; and *Bulletin of the Atomic Scientists*, Educational Foundation for Nuclear Science, 935 E. 50th St., Chicago, Ill.,ten times yearly, $8.50 yearly. *Defense Monitor*, published by the Center for Defense Information, a watch-dog service on military spending and operations headed by retired Admiral Gene R. La Rocque, 122 Maryland Avenue NE, Washington, DC 20002. The *Monitor* appears about five or six times a year. No charge!

War-Peace Report provides thorough coverage of the broad spectrum of the American peace movement. *Win* promotes the ideal of peace and freedom through non-violent action. *Fellowship* relates peace action to religious faith. *The Federalist* promotes world peace through world law. The *Bulletin of the Atomic Scientists* covers the world of science and its relationship to the peace process.

"Conscription is for slaves, not free men. These words do not come easily, but they are true and the truth needs saying. The truth, as clearly as one sees it, also needs acting upon." With these words Robert Eaton began his statement before the federal court in Phladelphia on August 27, 1969. He was being tried for refusing induction into the army. He had worked as a Quaker in North and South Vietnam and also with many of the underprivileged in American society. "We have learned that the beginning of construction has to be a clear 'No' to destruction," he stated and continued:

We find ourselves administering to an increasingly fossilized and violent society . . . established religion blesses nuclear submarines, legislatures outlaw flag burning in this country and finance child burning in Vietnam, courts back down on a solemn pledge at the Nuremburg and Tokyo war crimes trials to apply to our country the same standard of justice involving war crimes that we applied to the World War II enemies. [7]

A group of some 200 friends accompanied Bob Eaton to the courthouse. I was one of them.

By his act of refusing induction and all cooperation with the Selective Service System, Robert Eaton was saying the most effective "No" to killing that can be said. Leo Tolstoy in his book *The Kingdom of God Is Within You* has written that to refuse conscription is the strongest act that the individual can take against war. I agree with Tolstoy, not only because the young man who chooses prison rather than killing people sets an effective example, but also because he appeals to the most powerful force within the individual—his conscience.

Thousands of young Bob Eatons over the land who have said "No" to killing in Vietnam have done much to help recall America to her ideals. Since 1965, hundreds of thousands have applied for C.O. (over 100,000 in the single year 1970).[8] So influential was their impact on the war and on America that Clark Clifford, Secretary of Defense, told the Joint Chiefs that they could not have the increase in men that they asked. He said that the 36,000 C.O.'s that year showed that the country could not go on drafting men without limits. The Joint Chiefs said they needed one million more men to win and 200,000 to continue the war. Clifford told them that the example of the C.O.'s was evidence they could not get a million men. At that point the escalation of troops stopped. They did not get the 200,000. The influence of C.O.'s was substantial.

Besides the C.O.'s, many more are in prison or under indictment for acts which are indirectly connected with refusal of induction. One was arrested in Washington, D.C., for stealing a car. The draft board had refused his conscientious objector application and he discovered that he would be rejected by the army if he were arrested on a felony charge. He was rejected but the friend who advised them to steal the Volkswagon was arrested for advising theft.

Unknown numbers of soldiers in military prisons during the Vietnam War were there because they could not morally accept the war and follow orders, but found no other way of escaping it than to violate a minor rule, like going AWOL. Many of these were discharged from the military with less than honorable discharges to follow them the rest of their lives. From July 1961 to June 1973 there were 637,357 discharges of this kind. This does not include approximately 80,000 Americans who have left the country to take up residence in Canada, 400 in Sweden, and others in other hospitable Nations rather than consent to kill in Vietnam. These men have taken effective and direct action against the war; their actions have reached and touched the consciences of millions of other Americans.

Tax Resistance. "Why pay for a war you do not believe in?" is one of the slogans advocating tax refusal. Joan Baez, the famous folk singer, refuses to pay taxes. In 1964, she wrote to the Internal Revenue Service saying that she was not going to pay 60 per cent of her 1963 income tax. She gave two reasons:

It is enough to say that no man has the right to take another's life. Now we plan and build weapons that can take thousands of lives in one second, millions of lives in a day, billions in a week. My other reason is that modern war is impractical and is stupid. We spend billions of dollars a year on weapons which scientists, politicians, military men and even presidents all agree must never be used . . .[yet] people are starving to death in some places in the world. They look to this country with all its wealth and power. They look at our national budget. They are supposed to respect us. They despise us.

The government can attach your bank account, and force collection, but this does not erase the witness of your opposition to the killing in war. Today, 65 per cent of the federal tax dollar goes to war-related-expenses.[9] About 54 per cent goes to the present war machine. Some tax refusers do not pay 70 per cent, others 54 per cent.

The *Handbook on Non-payment of Taxes for War,* written by the members of the Peacemaker Movement, Greenmaker Books, Canterbury, New Hampshire, 1967, says: "Since 1948 when the non-payment movement began, only six persons have been brought before a commissioner or a U.S. District Court." This shows that the Internal Revenue Service has only occasionally forced collections from non-taxpayers.''

I think it is true to say that no one has been jailed for refusing to pay taxes. There have been jail sentences on charges of falsification of exemption claims; for example, when peace organizations or poor are claimed as exemptions. They could be jailed and must run the risk of jail if they refuse war taxes. But the government wisely tries to avoid making tax martyrs. They could become heroes and endanger the system. What the government wants is money, and this can be taken from bank accounts or confiscated property. In a word, if they do go to jail, their witness is more effective. The government does not want that.

It is quite clear, therefore, that if large numbers refused to pay because of their opposition to war, there would be a strong political effect on the government.

A smaller way of tax resistance is to refuse to pay the 10 per cent telephone tax to which Rep. Wilbur Mills referred when the 1966 law raising the telephone tax was under discussion. Congressman Mills said, "The Vietnam and only the Vietnam operation makes this bill necessary."[1] Refusal to pay that 10 per cent of the phone tax or surtax does not result in discontinuation of the phone service. The telephone company does not like the idea of the tax either.

The Internal Revenue Service can collect unpaid phone taxes in various ways. They can attach a bank account or put a lien against other property. However, they are not very active in doing this: the expense is great, the amount collected is small. Even if they do collect, you have forced them into extra work and especially into taking cognizance of your personal stand against war.

The War Resisters League estimates that there are now 20,000 people over the nation who refuse to pay the telephone tax. Additional information on all kinds of war resistance through taxes may be obtained by writing them at 339 Lafayette St., New York, N.Y., 10012.

Various Individual Actions. Dr. Benjamin Spock, undoubtedly the most famous baby doctor in the United States, perhaps in the world, showed what one man can do. He tried every legal way to stop the war. Finally, he urged the youth to resist the draft. He was arrested and tried for conspiracy to obstruct the Selective Service System.

Over the year of Dr. Spock's trial and appeal, the news of his resistance helped many Americans think critically about the war. Dr. Spock gave them the example of a man who put his prestige, his profession, his future on the line to express his conviction that he is just as interested in the eighteen- to twenty-year-old as he is in infants. With Dr. Spock, the Rev. William Sloan Coffin, a chaplain at Yale University, was indicted. During the period of his prosecution, the Reverend Coffin was strongly supported at Yale.

In the 1969 Yale graduation ceremony, a young student spoke against the war. Both Yale and Harvard and other schools in the spring of 1969 began to re-evaluate ROTC on campus. The example of men like the Reverend Coffin has had a strong effect on organizing this kind of response from the youth of the Ivy League colleges. These men and their companions also make thinking Americans wonder about our freedom of expression, about justice in our courts. Americans saw the courts refuse again and again to examine the war itself or the unconstitutional waging of an undeclared war. All of this helped create an aversion to judicial procedure in respect to this particular war.

A Catholic priest from Duluth, Minnesota, Philip Solem, wrote a letter to high school graduates of a Catholic school in Duluth urging them to resist induction. He gave reasons why he thought the Vietnam War was immoral as judged by the just-unjust war theory. Towards the end he wrote, "I ask you to read this letter carefully and consider what I say. By writing it I violate the Selective Service Act and risk a five-year jail sentence." He was verbally attacked by a large number of parents and students in the school, but 20 per cent of the student body, which was looking for religious leadership on the moral issue of war, turned to him with joy and enthusiasm. He spurred the Catholic community and the neighborhood in which he lived to think more deeply about the moral issues of the war. His witness has had an effect beyond Duluth on Catholics all over the United States and in the rest of the world. Had he escalated his letter writing and joined with other clergymen to reach the youth in many parts of the country, he might have been arrested for doing precisely what a clergyman should do: speak the truth on a moral issue. Had he been arrested for this, he would have received wide backing from the American public. His witness in jail would have been most effective in waking up the conscience of America to what we are doing in Vietnam.

Puerto Rican Bishop Antulio Parilla-Bonilla, speaking to thousands of students in the University of Puerto Rico in May 1969, urged the students and all others to refuse the draft. He said, "Refusal to serve in the army or in the armed forces of the United States, regardless of consequences of humiliation, jail or persecution, is a very efficacious form of protest."

A medical doctor, Captain Howard Levy, was court-martialed because he refused to continue teaching soldiers going to Vietnam. He contended that they were misusing the techniques he taught them to harm people instead of to help them. He was also accused by the army of disloyalty because he said that if he were a Negro, he would never fight in Vietnam. His refusal to use his medical knowledge to destroy people reached millions of Americans who read about his trial and his punishment. Present laws may even be changed because of the efforts he made to have the courts recognize the right of conscience, especially for medical doctors.

Captain Dale Noyd, professor of psychology at the

United States Air Force Academy, is another shining example of a man whose conscience helped all of us. For eighteen months he maintained that the war in Vietnam was unjust and he would not be a part of it. When he was ordered on December 4, 1968, to train a pilot in jet flying, he refused, since all of those trained went to Vietnam. Before this, he had requested and was denied conscientious objector status. He had requested and was denied reassignment or an opportunity to resign. In the course of his court-martial, Major Smith, the prosecutor, argued that "there must be a reasonable subordination of religious faith in military service." Captain Noyd, a religious humanist, believed that there were limits to what his conscience would allow him to do. He also contended that the Nuremberg principles bound the United States to respect his conscience. The court refused to listen and sentenced him for failing to obey an order.

Captain Noyd's story gave courage to officers and other men everywhere. His punishment was light, so this may also encourage others to follow his example. It may set new precedents for military law.

On April 12, 1968, a Marine court-martial sentenced Corporal Mary Elizabeth Burns for refusing to wear the Marine uniform. Back in her home-town, her twenty-four-year-old-twin brother, Tim, had already refused to take the step that would induct him into the United States Army.

Mary, whose job it was to forward radio messages from men in Vietnam to their families, after eighteen months of service, reached a point of realization of the inhumanity of the Marine Corps. She took her uniform to her Marine captain and informed the captain that she could no longer, in conscience, be a part of the Marines.

Despite pleas of her lawyer that she be given an administrative discharge, the military machine tried to grind her down with a court-martial. They soon found that the presence of a woman in the grinding machine did more harm to Marine prestige than it did to Mary. Finally, after the court-martial condemned her to confinement to barracks and a $20 fine, the Marine Corps, with egg all over its uniform, dismissed her with a general discharge.

John Fucillo of New York was drafted into the army after an unsuccessful appeal for conscientious objector status. He decided on his own personal system of confronting the army. He learned all the rules and observed them, but he fearlessly pointed out in a letter to his sergeant and to all his superior officers how the sergeant had failed to observe army rules by the way he talked and treated the men. When the lieutenant attacked John for his action, he wrote more letters complaining that the lieutenant did not wish army rules to be observed.

In the barracks, in public and in private, John spoke against the Vietnam War. He carefully observed all the rules, however. In nine months the army discharged him for not having a proper attitude.

He had confronted army officials with their own failures to live up to their own laws. It was lonely and difficult, but he believes that he brought to the attention of many army officials their own failures to follow the ideals that they preached. His additional witness to his freedom in speaking against foreign policy to all those around him made him undesirable company for the army.

Daniel Ellsburg, M.I.T. professor and Defense Department expert, risked a life in jail by giving the public the secret government appraisal of the Vietnam war called the Pentagon Papers. To block their continued printing, the Nixon administration appealed to the Supreme Court. The news of government deceit of its own people rocked the nation and did much to turn the tide against the war.

I asked Dan Ellsburg how he had the courage to do it. He replied, "I saw what others were forced to do to support the war. I saw what Vietnamese and Americans were suffering because of the war. I knew the war was wrong and these papers would show it. I believed the people should know the truth, so I did it to make the truth known.''

Don Dawson, a B52 pilot during the Christmas bombing of Cambodia, refused to fly. He had to stand almost alone against the military in which he was an officer. At the time Congress and most of the country were opposed to the invasion of Cambodia, but Mr. Nixon, as commander-in-chief, was ordering it. Don Dawson's refusal to fly strengthened those opposing Nixon. Dawson was discharged because the military feared the political effects of a public court-martial. But Dawson had to risk court-martial to give his good example.

Similar courage was shown by Major Hal Knight, Jr. of the U.S. Air Force who revealed before the Senate Armed Services Committee (July, 1973) the secret bombing of Cambodia which was illegal and about which the Nixon Administration and the Air Force had lied to the Congress. He himself had been a key supervisor in the bombing. His stand strengthened others.

Action of Two Priests. In Cleveland on January 26, 1969, two Roman Catholic priests were carried and dragged from the altar of St. John's Roman Catholic Cathedral. The newspapers showed the priests held by the police on the sidewalk. The priests were still in their liturgical vestments. They were taken to the jail in their vestments although they had requested the police to allow them to change clothes. After they were released from prison, still in the Mass vestments, they appeared in a television interview at the prison gates.

Robert T. Begin and Bernard L. Meyer, both priests of the Cleveland area, went into the Cathedral to offer Mass as a protest against the Catholic Church because it "coexists self-righteously and apathetically with immoral and inhuman wars, intolerable and divisive racism and extreme and dire poverty." Both the violence of the police and the disruption of the sacred ceremonies gave the Catholics of that area and of the entire United States reason to reflect.

A somewhat similar witness to the silence of organized religion about the war in Vietnam took place in front of the Shrine of the Immaculate Conception in Washington, D.C. As worshipers came out from their 1969 Holy Saturday ceremonies, an eight-foot crucifix was burned with napalm on the front steps in an antiwar protest. On the crucifix hung a black figure of Christ.

The Catholic Peace Fellowship, led by John Swinglish, organized this demonstration. They said it was "a protest to the lack of moral leadership" in society and the Roman Catholic Church. "By the burning of the paper Christ figure, we want to signify how Christ in man is being crucified in Vietnam."

Group Action

Many antiwar actions centered around the destruction of draft records. They began in 1969 when a nineteen-year-old Minnesotan, Barry Bondhaus, broke into his local draft board and dumped two large buckets of human feces into a filing cabinet, thereby mutilating several hundred 1-A draft records. Bondhaus, his eleven brothers, and his father, who had threatened to shoot anyone who attempted to induct any of his boys into the American army, had collected organic waste for two weeks in preparation for the raid.

By 1969, over sixty Americans awaited prison after destroying draft records by less rustic methods. The Baltimore 4, Philip Berrigan, James Mengal, David Eberherdt, and Thomas Lewis, poured blood on 600 draft records in October 1967.

In May 1968, Philip Berrigan, his priest brother Dan

and seven others, including a Catholic brother, a nurse, an artist, and two returned missionaries, destroyed draft files with homemade napalm at Catonsville, Maryland.

The Boston 2, students Suzi Williams and Frank Femia, mutilated draft records with black paint in June 1968.

The Milwaukee 14 napalmed some 10,000 draft records in September 1968.

The Pasadena 3, Silver Spring 3, Chicago 15, Women against Daddy Warbucks, and the New York 8 have all destroyed draft records.

The New York 8 destroyed some 75,000 records in the Bronx on August 1, 1969, and several thousand more at a Queens draft board on August 15. Among the four men and four women, there were three Catholic priests.

Statements were made by the groups to explain why they did these actions. They prayed and had some liturgical ceremony while they waited to be arrested. They voluntarily accepted imprisonment to reach the conscience of other Americans.

The Catonsville 9 statement reads in part as follows:

We use napalm on these draft records because napalm has burned people to death in Vietnam, Guatemala and Peru; and because it may be used on America's ghettos.... We believe some property has no right to exist: Hitler's gas ovens, Stalin's concentration camps, atomic, bacteriological and chemical weaponry, files of conscription.... We are Catholic Christians who take the Gospel of our faith seriously.

The Camden 28 were led on to enter and destroy draft files by an FBI informer after they had decided against doing so. Their long trial during which the informer clearly admitted his spy role for the FBI helped the country to understand how the government tried to entrap those who opposed it. On that basis the jury returned with a "not guilty" verdict. The trial converted even the informer.

During the last 45 days of the bombing of Cambodia 162 people were arrested for pray-ins at the White House They entered day after day with the tourists and were arrested when they remained to pray. Their willingness to suffer jail encouraged others and gave newsmen a focus for news opposing the bombing.

As the U.S. withdrew troops and began using the electronic battlefield technique in Vietnam, Jim Douglas professor at University of Hawaii, went with his friend into the Air Force Headquarters at Hawaii and poured his own blood on the files. All the computerized bombing was directed from this headquarters. Jim was severely beaten and dragged down the stairs by an Air force officer. At the trial the Air Force refused to show the records, so the charge was dropped.

A characteristic of all these acts is that utmost care was taken that no injury was done to human persons.

Many of the participants were older Americans, not just youth. They represented prestigious positions in society teachers, clergymen, nuns. They were people who were safe from the war, but people who identified themselves with the struggle and the suffering of the young. All this added strength to their witness and confronted America with public court cases to force reflection on what we were doing and why. At the Catonsville trial, Judge Thomsen said. "You may be found right by history or philosophy."

The tactic of destruction of property will be unacceptable to many who wish to work for peace However, according to traditional Christian morality, a law can and should morally be disobeyed when:

1. The law conflicts with a higher law, for example, a law that orders a person to kill another.

2. The disobedience to law comes as a last resort after petition and all other legal and organized efforts have failed.

3. Those who commit the act of civil disobedience are

able to show in their lives a pattern of deep respect for law. This makes it clear that their act is not an attack on law in general, but merely on the immorality or unjustness of a particular law.

4. Those who commit such civil disobedience in order to show their deep respect for law willingly accept the punishment for what they consider to be an innocent act and appeal to society to judge the immorality of the law for which they are punished.

5. In disobeying the law, they do not harm any human person.

I think that all of these principles apply to antidraft acts better than they apply to the American colonists who dressed themselves up as Indians and poured tea into Boston Harbor. Those "heroes" did not stay to take the punishment; they dressed as Indians; they helped start a bloody revolution.

Some of the leaders of the War Resisters League, like Jim Peck and Dave McReynolds, think that antiwar actions involving secrecy, property destruction, and "elitism" (a small group acting without democratic and open appeal to the masses of the people) will hurt the peace movement in the long run. They argue that such tactics do not fully follow the Gandhian theory of non-violence. They also say that such actions will be repaid by far rightist anger and vengeance. These arguments deal with tactics: they do not touch the moral issue.

The Berrigans and others do not claim that their's was the best action. They do claim that they said "NO" to war at a very high price to themselves and with no personal harm to any others. They wanted their example to move others to act against the war in whatever way suited their own consciences.

More Conventional Group Action. The Quakers belong

to a peace Church which has made its mark on American history. William Penn, a Quaker, gave his name to the state founded by a group of Quakers. From the earliest days in their dealings with the Indians, the Quakers refused to take part in killing. Among the Christian communities they are one of the "peace Churches."

Through the American Friends Service Committee Quakers have worked in Vietnam, Nigeria, and Biafra to meet the needs of civilian war sufferers. This service includes medical and rehabilitation services for amputees. Throughout the war, they have collected funds for the victims of war. They have organized visitations to prisoners of conscience in American federal prisons.

Through the Quaker Action Group names of the war dead were read on the steps of the Capitol in June 1969. Throughout summer months, groups of people, including Congressmen, challenged the country to remember these dead. They were briefly arrested for this activity and then released.

The Quakers have camps for training in non-violence. There they research issues on war and peace; they print and distribute information. The American Friends Service Committee believes that each human life is sacred, that each man is a child of God. They believe that love expressed through creative action, can overcome hatred, prejudice, and fears. Seeking non-violent ways of solving conflict, they welcome help from all interested people.

War Resisters League. The War Resisters League is part of an international resistance against all types of war. (The American headquarters is at 339 Lafayette St., New York, N.Y., 10012.) The league strives for close cooperation with all peace organizations in the hopes of encouraging individuals and groups to renounce war once and for all, to find non-violent solutions for conflict, to withdraw from the political power struggle, and to work for a social order based on non-violence. The League holds conferences, seminars, study-work camps, and campaigns against militarism, conscription, violence, and injustice.

Fellowship of Reconciliation. This organization of 14,000 members began in 1914. It describes itself as a

fellowship of individuals who recognize the essential unity of mankind and who have come together to explore the power of love and truth for resolving human conflict ... they identify with those of every nation, race and religion who are the victims of injustice and exploitation, and seek to develop resources of active, non-violent intervention with which to help rescue them ... they strive to build a social order that will utilize the resources of human ingenuity and wisdom to the benefit of all men.

Branches of the Fellowship are The Catholic Peace Fellowship, The Episcopal Peace Fellowship and The Jewish Peace Fellowship.

Some widely known organizations (The American Civil Liberties Union, The Congress of Racial Equality, and The American Committee on Africa) came into existence through the efforts of the Fellowship of Reconciliation.

Allied with the Fellowship of Reconciliation is the Catholic Peace Fellowship and the Episcopal and Jewish Peace Fellowships. These try to move their own groups towards peacemaking. The Fellowship has headquarters at Nyack, N.Y., P.O. Box 271. There it conducts an extensive mail order service of books and pamphlets related to its work.

The Catholic Worker Movement. This group for forty years has opposed war, fed the poor through hospitality houses, and promoted peace. Through communal living, the practice of voluntary poverty, the monthly publication of *The Catholic Worker* (.01 cents a copy) it has tried to humanize life.

Its founder, Dorothy Day, has probably done more to move the Roman Catholic Church to action for peace than any other person. Thousands of priests, bishops, nuns, and seminarians have visited the Catholic Worker hospitality house at 36 1st Ave., New York. Through them and others the movement has reached the nation.

Pax Christi, USA. This organization is part of an international Catholic peace group headed by Cardinal Alfrink of Holland. Bishops Dozier of Memphis and Gumbleton of Detroit are the moderators in the USA. It aims to promote peace through the Catholic structure.
Gen. Sec. Dr. Joseph Fahey, Pax Christi, Manhattan College, Riverdale, N.Y. 10471.

Pax Christi, USA. Newsletter can be obtained from Gerard A. Vanderhaar, Editor, Christian Brothers' College, Memphis, TN 38104.

National Peace Academy Campaign. A nonpartisan, public interest campaign to establish a Federal Educational institution to promote peace. The USA has established four military academies and five war colleges. The time has come to establish a National Academy for Peace. To do this we can support Senate Bill 469 introduced by Senators Randolph and Hatfield and H.R. 2651 introduced by Cong. Andrew Young with nine co-sponsors to create a Peace Academy Commission, January 1977.

CCCO. The Central Committee for Conscientious Objectors, founded in 1948, is independent, non-profit and non-sectarian. CCCO looks forward to the time when our society will no longer have conscription. It is dedicated to helping those confronted by the draft. It also assists men and women in the military who can no longer in good conscience carry arms. They publish a newsletter for $3 per year and *Handbook for Conscientious Objectors* and other self-help books. The main office is: 2016 Walnut St., Philadelphia, PA 19103.

Clergy and Laymen Concerned About Vietnam. This is a national emergency committee, formed about 1965, to express the moral concern of clergy and others with regard to the Vietnam War. It is interdenominational and has a broad following of clergy and laymen throughout the country. (The address is 475 Riverside Dr., New York, N.Y., 10027.) It works with many national peace groups and promotes programs of amnesty, reconciliation with Vietnam, Bread for the World.

UNA-USA. The United Nations Association is a cooperative alliance of more than one hundred national voluntary organizations for information and educational activities about the United Nations.

UNA-USA is dedicated to strengthening our country's capacity for advancing peace, freedom, and justice in the world through the development of the United Nations and other international organizations. Working in research, information, and educational fields, it cooperates with foundations and universities. Supported entirely by contributions from individuals and organizations, it is independent and non-partisan. (Its headquarters are at 345 E. 46th St., New York, N.Y. 10017.)

The World Federalists. The World Federalists organization believes in a world federal government. It seeks to convince the people that a world federal government is essential to human survival and that such a government would preserve our basic freedoms. It feels this can be achieved by orderly constitutional means. It has a program for World Peace Through World Law with headquarters at The Hague. It also has an office at 1346 Conn. Ave., NW., Washington, D.C., 20036.

The World Federalists organization is a voluntary, non-partisan group supported by dues from many thousands of thoughtful Americans. It has branches throughout the country and works through discussion groups and talks to build wider support for its ideals.

These are just some of the many and varied organizations that work for peace. There are many others. The SANE Nuclear Policy Committee (381 Park Avenue So., New York, N.Y. 10016) promotes peaceful change. SANE has local branches in many cities. The Center for Defense Information, 122 Maryland Avenue NE, Washington, DC 20002, is a civilian watchdog group on Pentagon spending and policy. It publishes an occasional bulletin, *The Defense Monitor*. COPRED, Consortium of Peace Research, Education and Development, is a federation of over 90 US peace institutes, most of them in universities. Its headquarters is at Gustavus Adolphus College, St. Peter, Minn. 56082.

In most communities there are peace centers, like the Washington Peace Center and the Philadelphia Peace Center. These all welcome volunteers. In Washington, D.C., there is also the National Committee to Repeal the Draft.

Government or Public Action. One basic form of public action would be to support Senate Resolution 185, a bill introduced by Senator McGovern and some thirty-one other Senators calling for a reconversion of the economy to a peacetime economy. Senator McGovern first made this proposal in 1963. It was then cosponsored by twenty-nine of his Senate Colleagues. Hearings were held by the Commerce Committee in 1964, but the buildup of the Vietnam War lessened interest in the bill. Because it is a problem for the government to convert its spending from military to civilian goals, this bill asking for a change of priorities needs every kind of backing: educational support, lobbying, support for those politicians who are behind it. The bill needs the election of more men who will back it. The World Peace Tax Fund Bill is sponsored by Congressman Ron Dellums of California, and over 23 other Congresspeople. It would allow conscientious objectors, and those opposed to war for reasons of faith and conscience to put the war portion of their taxes in a special peace fund. More information is available from the Council for a World Peace Tax Fund at 2111 Florida Avenue, NW, Washington, D.C. 20008.

We need a change in foreign policy. We should cease serving as "policeman of the world" and protector of invested interests and become the nation promoting world security on an international basis. In this, the United States would play a major role, but one subordinate to an international organization with international interests.

This means an end to the negative anti-Communist, anti-revolutionary interventionism that characterizes our present foreign policy. It means that we must understand that peace must be based on justice. Pope Paul calls *development* and *cooperation* the new words for peace. This peace must be on the economic, political, and social level and must reach to the individual. That is, it must recognize human rights.

The achievement of peace involves, as Tom Stonier says, "the evolution of a constellation of attitudes and institutions, each reinforcing the other so as to construct an ever enlarging community of international law, justice and therefore world order."

To make this clear to those in the Church, in the classroom, on the street corner is a job for everyone. It is a job involving a reevaluation of our present institutions and the evolution of new institutions. Among these could be a Peace Academy, a Department of Peace, a course on peace in every college and university, reversal of the glorification of war in secondary and elementary textbooks, films, and entertainment.

To accomplish this on the political front will mean the election of candidates who have an international outlook. To get them elected will require the creation of that international outlook among the populace. One way is to strengthen the prestige and power of the United Nations. Instead of criticizing the UN, we might better study it and see the limitations we impose when we bypass it in the Vietnam War. How can we expect effectiveness with this example?

One interested in seeing the UN succeed might ask: "Could the U.S. have done more to stop the Arab-Israeli conflict in 1956, the Congo-Katanga conflict in 1964-66 and the Cyprus civil war in 1963?" This question acknowledges the peace-keeping work of the UN in preventing World War III. It might also show the need for strengthening the UN.

Improvements are easy to suggest: an end to the "veto"—how can the UN function when a single power can block it?; representation proportionate to the population represented; Article 43 revised to provide a more capable standby force. A larger number of nations should contribute peace-keeping forces and funds for peace-keeping action. Closer bonds between the UN and regional groups like NATO could be established.

The United States could vastly increase its financial help to the UN. It could start to train and supply some of its forces for UN duty; especially needed are transportation, communication, and logistic support. Seven countries now have designated units of their armed forces for emergency duty with the UN. We could train men for UN duty in our colleges or in a United States Peace Academy, replacing ROTC. We could work for the cession of all deep-water rights to the UN. The same UN control could apply to outer space.

We could help develop an international outlook by the abolition of all travel restrictions, by the recognition of all countries that have had a de facto existence of five years or more.

We could work toward the increase of effectiveness and cooperation between such institutions as the Postal Union and air safety and scientific institutions.

If even some of this were done, we would find nuclear and conventional arms control easier and disarmament more attainable.

Disarmament

We should realize that disarmament is more difficult for a totalitarian government like the Soviet Union than it is for us. Disarmament requires inspection and an openness and a yielding of some sovereignty. Even we find that difficult.

To work toward disarmament a knowledge of the record of efforts that have been made in disarmament and how they have failed is needed. Such knowledge would show us that no nation is guiltless. The record also shows that something can be done. The Test Ban Treaty and Nuclear Non-proliferation Treaty were passed. This is some progress, even though we are still far from total and mutual disarmament.

The paradoxically hopeful aspect for disarmament is that we all face the same problem: survival in a nuclear world. Survival is not just the morality of one religion or political system. Since everyone wants to survive, and since peace is essential for survival, then perhaps this may be the first time peace is really possible.

Chapter 5

HOPES AND FEARS
IN OUR FUTURE

"I think I know what is bothering the students. I think I know what we are up against. It is a generation that is by no means sure that it has a future," said Nobel Prize winning laureate Dr. George Wald. He was speaking to some 1200 scientists, students and others gathered in Kresge Auditorium at the Massachusetts Institute of Technology. He "talked extemporaneously—his head back, his eyes almost closed." His words had an electric effect. A hush fell over the audience. A well-known lecturer of biology, he talked of the issues that he felt bothered the students: a draft system that had been with them all their lives, an overgrown defense establishment, the threat of nuclear destruction and, in the last few years, the tragedy of the Vietnam war. [1]

I did not need to read the words of Dr. Wald to know that the students feel this way. I teach at Georgetown University: I meet many students from other universities. I have been consulted by young men who are wondering about leaving America, about whether there is any hope for a future here. I met a young couple who decided that it would be immoral to bring children into a world as dangerous and insane as this one.

This mood of the students was expressed at the June 12, 1969 Harvard Commencement by a law student, Melvin E. Levine: "I have asked many of my classmates what they wanted me to say today. 'Talk with them about hypocrisy,' most of them said. 'Tell them they have broken the best heads in the country, embittered the most creative minds and turned off their most talented scholars.'[2] 'Tell them they have destroyed our confidence and lost our respect'."

At the Yale graduation in June of 1969, William McIlwane Thompson, the senior class secretary, said, "Today despair outweighs hope, mourning outweighs celebration. The war is destroying not one nation, but two—the Vietnamese and our own. Our cities are in decay; our universities are in chaos; our poor are hungry. And yet our money and our energies are expended upon war and the perpetuation of war. Today as we leave Yale, a sense of frustration and despair overwhelms us."[3]

Students are not the only ones who see nuclear clouds in their futures. A group of nuclear experts from Harvard and MIT concluded that nuclear war by 1999 is probable. They make the following points:

1) It will probably occur as the direct result of the spread of nuclear power and nuclear weapons.

2) The existing political systems continue to increase their stockpiles of nuclear weapons.

3) To control weapons, nations would have to surrender much of their sovereignty: yet they show no sign of being willing to do that.

Richard Garwin, a visiting professor of physics at Harvard says, "The Atomic Energy Commission once had total control of our weapons. Long ago they were ceded to the Department of Defense. The basing of many weapons on foreign territory under our nominal control increases the chance of unauthorized use either by U.S. personnel or others." [4]

George B. Kistiakowsky, a Harvard chemist, former chief of the explosives division of Los Alamos Laboratories says, "There has never been a case in history of an arms race ending by laying down of arms. As the military acquires more and more weapons, it will acquire more and more power: and the military tends to resolve conflicts by military means." [5]

George Rathjens, professor at MIT, has worked on the advanced research project agency for the Department of Defense says, "Each large reactor is now producing enough material to build a weapon a week, and predictions are that by the end of the century there will be several thousand reactors around the world." [6]

Thomas Schelling of Harvard, consultant to the Departments of State and Defense says, "I used to think that one of the most horrendous facts I ever heard was the number of American nuclear weapons stationed on foreign soil. But, confronted with the number of weapons that could be made per week by 1999 from the fissionable products of non-military reactors, I am beginning to believe that proliferation (like billions of mosquitoes hatching out of billions of eggs) means infection and is a concern to be dealt with like matters of public health." [7]

Garwin says the budget of the Arms Control and Disarmament Agency is "less than 1/10,000 of the Defense Department's. For every dollar that goes into that agency, ten thousand are going into the Pentagon." [8]

These prestigious scientists have watched the U.S. arsenal grow until it now has over 30,000 nuclear weapons; 8,000 strategic (large) and 22,000 tactical weapons (smaller); each 3 to 5 times the size of the Hiroshima bomb. The tactical weapons are based mostly overseas. The total yield of these bombs combined is 600 thousand times the explosive power of the bomb that destroyed Hiroshima. By 1982 there will be 100,000 nuclear weapons in the world. The Stockholm International Peace Research Institute predicts, ''About 35 countries will be able to make atomic weapons within 9 years....and nuclear war will become inevitable.''

The United States has about 40 H-bombs strategically targeted at every major Soviet city with a population of 100,000 or more. One bomb delivered would destroy the city. After that the dust could be stirred 39 times. The Soviet Union could destroy every American city of 100,000 or over and then raise the radioactive dust on each of those cities 13 more times; with 13 more bombs for each city. Niether the U.S. nor the USSR has any way of defending itself against these bombs in the foreseeable future.

A terrorist group capable of making a nuclear weapon would need to hijack only ten pounds of plutonium to make four bombs. A Princeton student designed such weapons, with college level nuclear physics knowledge last year. Such a weapon could be set off in the desert to prove possession, and then downtown areas of three cities could be held hostage. If these bombs were manufactured abroad they could easily be smuggled into the United States.

Opposed to all this build-up with its immense economic and political support there are signs of hope. Wes Michaelson in SOJOURNERS of February 1977 says, ''The bomb finds its rationale only in the idolatry of nationhood which condemns millions to death in the name of its survival. Relegating the state to its proper biblical role, and yielding our primary loyalty to Christ's kingdom necessitates the abolition of the bomb.''

Some increased recognition of this truth shows itself in the willingness of the Catholic community to speak truth to power. In Detroit the U.S. Catholic community in its Call to Action statement asks "that in the light of consistent church teaching on modern warfare, the U.S. Catholic community condemn, and be among those who lead in resisting the production, possession, proliferation and threatened use of nuclear weapons and all other weapons of indiscriminate effect, even in a policy of deterrence..." [9]

In South Africa Catholic Bishops openly and publicly have opposed the unjust racial laws of the white minority government. In Rhodesia Bishop Donal Lamont was condemned to jail for giving medical help to a wounded guerilla; and was later exiled. In El Salvador in July, 1977, 42 Jesuit priests threatened with death if they did not get out of the country by a set date of July 21, refused to leave. They were supported by their bishops and by the Jesuit order. The Atlantic Life Community, The Great Lakes Life Community, and the Pacific Life Community actively organized to oppose the development of the Trident and other missile systems. They have repeatedly suffered imprisonment for their faith-based witness to the value of life, and their condemnation of the idolatry of the bomb. In Baltimore, Maryland, the Jonah House Community leads the way in this witness. On the Pacific coast near Bangor, Washington, a coalition of Americans and Canadians led the witness to life at the Trident base.

In the United States a branch of the International Pax Christi became nationally visible under the leadership of Bishop Carroll Dozier of Memphis, Tennessee. (He was the first Catholic Bishop to strongly and clearly condemn the immorality of the Vietnam war with a pastoral letter). Pax Christi now has 17 Catholic Bishop members and tries to move the Catholic Church toward faithfulness and towards its own peace gospel. This has shown itself in increased peace education programs and an increased acceptance of the peace voices in the church.

The victory of the coalition of peace groups in stopping the B-1 bomber after many years of well organized work, marks the first time in the history of the United States that a major weapons system has been stopped. This was done through long-range education at the grass roots level. It included lobbying, obtaining a campaign pledge from Jimmy Carter, and urging him to be true to his campaign word after election. Although this victory was partially offset by the turning to the cruise missile as an alternative, it shows that determined action on the political level can be effective.

This had already been done in a larger way in stopping the Vietnam war with the consequent and connected ousting of Nixon from office. Every one of the many massive and small acts of resistance to that war coalesced to accomplish that. Every act was needed and was effective.

The cruise missile is described in the Defense Monitor for September, 1976, as a miniature unmanned airplane that can be launched from submarines or surface ships or other airplanes such as the B-52s. Evidence of American high technology, the cruise missile is a mechanical marvel that can fly under computer control close to the ground to avoid enemy radar detection. It guides itself with great precision to its target and has a range of 2500 miles.

Another hopeful sign was the coalition of Peace groups and environmentalists that occupied the Seabrook, N.H. reactor plant site in May of 1977. About 1,500 persons chose to go to jail rather than leave the property, a witness to the truth that it is better to be active today than radio-active tomorrow. The 1,500 submitting to voluntary arrest made it one of the largest arrests through non-violent action in U.S. history. (The May Day arrests in

D.C. during the Vietnam war were larger.) Many people in this witness had never opposed the government or been arrested before. They were not only opposing a police order to leave a nuclear construction site, they were opposing the greed of the utility companies that threatens their futures and the futures of their children with dangerous radiation. Many of these people could not be termed radicals, they simply saw that all else they had tried, such as working through legal channels, did not work.

The importance of this action may be very great for the future. Those who come to understand what radio-activity means cannot be far from understanding what the bomb means. In fact as the Harvard and MIT scientists pointed out, there is a very close connection between them. Plutonium, which is the waste product of the reactors, can be reprocessed to make weapons. The fast reactor, the breeder reactor, will speed up the process. On the hopeful side President Carter has opposed the construction of the U.S. reprocessing plant at Clinch River.

Until this large protest developed it seemed that the separation of the peaceful atom and the atoms of war had been accomplished. This separation shows up now as an illusion.

President Carter gave us much hope in his inauguration speech when he called for zero nuclear weapons.

On the fearful side is the president's go-ahead on the neutron bomb. Developed secretly with 1.5 billion dollars of public works money the neutron bomb kills by concentrated radiation without much damage to property. This bomb tends to blur the separation between conventional and nuclear weapons. It tempts the military to promote the illusion that nuclear war is possible; that a limited nuclear war will not grow larger.

Also on the fearful side is the U.S. change in its policy

on nuclear war. Before 1975 the policy was mutually assured destruction, (MAD). If nuclear weapons were used, the U.S. would not be the first to use them. That has now been replaced by plans for limited nuclear war and for first strike nuclear capability, through the creation of a new counterforce nuclear policy. The U.S. has reversed its policy that it would not be the first to use the nuclear bomb. On May 30, 1975, Secretary Schlesinger admitted that the U.S. favors first use of nuclear weapons. That statement was backed up by Gerald Ford and has since been reaffirmed by Jimmy Carter.

Also on the fearful side is the development of the Trident submarine. It is an underwater monster as long as two football fields (560 feet), that can travel 40 miles per hour under water. It will carry 24 missiles capable of delivering 17 warheads with maneuverable re-entry capacity that makes them very accurate. The missiles have a range of 4,000 nautical miles. This gives Trident a capacity to destroy 408 cities each with a nuclear weapon which would be five times larger than the Hiroshima bomb. All this death and destruction will be under the control of one submarine commander. According to Robert Aldrich, a former Trident engineer, it will give the U.S. first strike capability. He calls it "the most lethal weapon ever built." [10]

On the hopeful side it is becoming more evident that the arms race is being fueled by the desire for profit and security for a few. Janet Aldrich, the wife of Robert, describing the struggle of her husband and herself to leave the security of a job with Lockheed after 16 years says, "The real motive behind the arms race gradually surfaced in our understanding; profits for the company and job security for the workers." [11] It is that fear of financial insecurity that is the block to all moral action in today's society. Once this is seen and recognized as the cause of the arms race rather than patriotism or defense of freedom, there is more hope that people who want peace will refuse to go along with it.

Even as this is being printed the Mobilization for Survival is getting under way. This is a campaign supported by a broad spectrum of political, labor, social, cultural and religious groups. It aims to end the production, testing and possession of nuclear weapons; to ban nuclear power; to stop the arms race and to fund human needs. This is the first national effort formed on ending our doomsday danger. Beginning August '77, with Hiroshima/Nagasaki Day actions, it will go until June '78, with teach-ins, speak-outs, appeals to local governments and Congress, and mass demonstrations.

Finally on the very hopeful side there is the leadership of women in the Community of Peace People in Northern Ireland. After the August 1976 death of three children caught in the para-military violence of Belfast, women began to demand an end to the killing. They marched and posted their peace declarations in their homes. They adopted non-violent action as their means. Their strength was based on their faith in God. This was the first time in human history that a national peace effort brought these elements together— 1) Leadership of women, 2) Non-violence, 3) Faith base. They offer a model to the world. If they can stop the 800 years of killing in Ireland, (and I think they can) then the women in Israel and Arab lands can do the same; so can the women in the U.S.S.R. and the U.S.A.

Here is the declaration of the Peace People. [12]

Dedication of a Peace Person
I have a simple message for the world from this movement for peace.

I want to live and love and build a just and peaceful society.

I want for children, as I want for myself, life at work, at home and at play to be a life of joy and peace.

I recognize that to build such a life demands of me dedication, hard work and courage.

I recognize that there are many problems in my society which are a source of conflict and violence.

I recognize that every bullet fired and every exploding bomb makes that work more difficult.

I reject the bomb and the bullet and all the techniques of violence.

I dedicate myself to working with my neighbors, near and far, day in and day out, to building that peaceful society in which the tragedies we have known are a bad dream and a continuing warning.

CONCLUSION

There is much reason to hope. With faith in God's help, with the good will and organization of good people, peace is possible. As Tolstoy says, "If evil people get together to do evil things, all that is needed is for good people to get together to do good things." The odds are formidable but threats that have come by human efforts can be put aside by human efforts.

From the analysis of technology or from a moral base, we come to the same conclusion. George Rathjens of MIT voices the technological view. "It does seem to me that when we discovered fission and decided to exploit it, we may have made inevitable the radical change in our whole mode of existence. A possible long term solution may well require a radical change in our whole life style ..." What he means, I think, is this: if we are not to destroy each other with the weapons of our own hands we must begin to cooperate together on this planet. Technology has brought us so close together that we cannot ignore each other. We must cooperate or die. No longer can we seek peace with any hope of finding it through war. The ancient truth that we never were able to find peace through war is now clear.

The gospel teaches us the same. We are all children of the one God with the obligation of loving one another. We should have learned that from our faith. We can now learn the same thing from technology. We can not treat others as though their destinies and our own are not related. Technology has been a help to us. It helps us to see what we believe by faith. What we believe by faith we believe without seeing. What we know from technology we know without faith. Put knowledge and faith together and we have more reason to hope than to fear.

Notes

NUCLEAR DISASTER

1. Thomas Stonier, *The War That Is Forbidden* (New York: Pax Publications, n.d.), p. 14.

2. Norman Cousins, *In Place of Folly* (New York: Washington Square Press, 1964), p. 14.

3. Harrison Brown and James Real, *Community of Fear* (Santa Barbara: Center for the Study of Democratic Institutions, 1967), p. 15.

4. Thomas Stonier, *Nuclear Disaster* (New York: Pax Publications, 1963), p. 77.

5. *Ibid.*, p. 22.

6. Philip Berrigan, *A Punishment for Peace* (New York: Macmillan, 1969), p. 129.

7. See *The Washington Post,* Feb. 2, 1968.

8. "The Defense Monitor", Vol. I No. 4, Sept. 8, 1972. 122 Maryland Ave. NE, Washington, DC 20002.

9. *Stockholm International Peace Research Institute Yearbook,* 1970, quoted in *New York Times,* Nov. 3, 1970.

10. "The Nuclear Time Bomb: Report to the UN Secretary," *Saturday Review,* Dec. 9, 1967, p. 19.

11. Seymour Hersh, *Chemical and Biological Warfare* (Indianapolis: Bobbs Merrill, 1968), p. 45.

12. Hersh, "Germs and Gas as Weapons," *New Republic,* June 7, 1969.

13. Hersh, *Chemical and Biological Warfare,* p. 108.

14. Ibid., p. 127.

15. Cousins, *In Place of Folly,* p. 73.

16. Mike Wallace Show, CBS, July 8, 1969.

17. Ibid.

18. Hersh, *Chemical and Biological Warfare,* p. 110.

19. *Bulletin of Atomic Scientists,* Sept. 1968, p. 68.

THE EXAMPLE OF CHRIST AND TODAY'S CONVENTIONAL WISDOM

1. Ronald Bainton, *Christian Attitudes Towards War and Peace,* pp. 66-84.

2. A possible exception is the US Catholic Bishops 1971 statement on Vietnam.

3. *Peace on Earth,* par. 114 (NCWC translation).

4. *Ibid.,* para. 158.

5. *Ibid.*

6. *Council Daybook* (Washington: United States Catholic Conference, 1965), I, 315; II, 172.

7. Gordon Zahn, "The Christian Vocation of Peace," *Ave Maria,* May 23, 1968, p. 6.

8. *Catholic Standard and Times,* Philadelphia, August 14, 1969.

9. The intention of the United States to reply with massive destruction is our deterrent strategy. See the statement of Secretary of Defense, Robert McNamara, on September 18, 1967. Our policy, McNamara contended, means that if attacked we intend to destroy not merely military forces but the aggressors's "society as a whole." This puts U.S. policy directly in conflict with the condemnation by Vatican II of acts of war "aimed indiscriminately at the destruction of entire cities or extensive areas."

10. "Puerto Rican Bishop Urges Draft Refusal," *National Catholic Reporter,* May 7, 1969, p. 1.

11. Constitution on the Church in the Modern World, par. 82.

12. *The Washington Post,* Oct. 5, 1965, sec. A, p. 12.

13. Constitution of the Church in the Modern World, par. 79.

14. *Congressional Record,* January 14, 1814.

15. *Congressional Record,* 65th Congress, Senate, p. 1078.

16. *Congressional Record,* 65th Congress, House, p. 974.

17. Army Chief of Staff, Annual Report for 1932.

18. *Congressional Record,* vol. 86, part 10. p. 11396.

19. *Ibid.,* p. 10487.

20. The boards paid little attention to the Seeger decision until 1970 when the court reaffirmed and enlarged it in the Welsh decision. At the time, with the war so unpopular, public attention forced the selective service system to incorporate the changes demanded by the court. Application form No. 150 used by CO applicants was changed only then to include the new decisions.

CONVENTIONAL WAR TODAY

1. Phillip Berrigan, *Punishment for Peace* (New York: Macmillan, 1969), p. 120.

2. New York: Harper&Bros., 1961.

3. New York: Bantam, 1967.

4. *Ibid.,* p. 103.

5. *Ibid.,* p. 45.

6. Senate speech, April 25, 1967.

7. *New York Times,* March 30, 1954.

8. The Pentagon Papers showed that the U.S. deliberately deceived the people on the Tonkin Gulf incident.

9. "Relief and rehabilitation of war victims in Indochina: one year after the cease-fire", Jan. 27, 1974. Office of Senator Kennedy.

10. *Ibid.*

11. For 1965-73, "The Impact of the Vietnam War", a report prepared for the Committee on Foreign Relations of the U.S. Senate, June 30, 1971, by the Congressional Research Service, Library of Congress. Also see, *Six Million Victims: the Human Cost of the Vietnam War under President Nixon,* prepared by Project Air War, 1322 18th St., NW, Washington, DC 20036.

12. *Congressional Record,* Feb. 16, 1966, p. 2927.

13. *Ibid.,* Feb. 8, 1968.

14. "Human Toll of War" prepared by U.S. Senate Subcommittee on Refugees, Sen. Edward Kennedy, Chairperson.

15. Primary sources: Pentagon Information Office and U.S. Subcommittee on Refugees. For Phoenix program Saigon Ministry of Information. These document the figures in this paragraph. also see footnote #11 above.

16. Cross Currents, Summer, 1966, p. 258.

THE PROCESS OF PEACE

1. Richard N. Goodwin, *Triumph or Tragedy: Reflections on Vietnam* (New York: Random House, 1966) pp. 64, 67.

2. Inscription on Jefferson's Monument in the Jefferson Memorial, Washington, D.C.

3. 1971 Statistical Abstract #405, #409, #364.

4. *Army Information Digest,* September, 1962, p. 38.

5. See bibliography.

6. See Chapter Two of the book for detailed information.

7. *Congressional Record,* House Hearings on Amnesty, Mar. 8, 11, 15, 1974, p. 609.

8. For more information on tax resistance see: *Ain't Gonna Pay for War No More* by Robert Calvert. Available from National Interreligious

Board for Conscientious Objectors, 550 Washington Bldg. 15th and NY Aves. NW, Wash, DC 20005. Cost $1.50.

9. See p. 74.

10. *Congressional Record*, February 23, 1966. The phone tax was due to end by 1974, but on January 2, 1971, Congress extended it at 10% until 1972. It will drop one percentage point each year until it expires in 1982.

HOPES AND FEARS IN OUR FUTURE

1. *New Yorker*, March 22, 1969 45: 29-31.
2. *New York Times*, June 13, 1969, p. 30.
3. *New York Times*, June 10, 1969, p. 49.
4. Washington Post, January 4, 1976. Section F, p. 4.
5. *Ibid.*
6. *Ibid.*
7. *Ibid.*
8. *Ibid.*
9. Call to Action, U.S. Catholic Conference, 1312 Mass. Ave, NW, Washington, DC. See Chapter Humankind, Section 3.
10. Sojourners, Feb. 1977, p. 4.
11. *Ibid.*, p. 31.
12. The Community of Peace People of Ireland, 8 Crescent Rd., Belfast, N. Ireland.

Bibliography

NUCLEAR WEAPONS

Bennett, John. *Nuclear Weapons and the Conflict of Conscience.* New York: Scribner's, 1962.

Cousins, Norman. *In Place of Folly.* New York: Washington Square Press Books, 1964, paper.

Hersh, Seymour, *Chemical and Biological Warfare: America's Hidden Arsenal.* Indianapolis: Bobbs Merrill, 1968.

King-Hall, Stephen, *Defense in the Nuclear Age.* Nyack, N.Y. Fellowship Publications, 1959.

Stonier, Thomas. *Nuclear Disaster.* New York: Doubleday Anchor, 1968.

THEORISTS ON VIOLENCE AND NON-VIOLENCE

Gandhi, M.K. *Non-violent Resistance.* New York: Schocken, 1961, paper.

Tolstoy, Leo. *The Kingdom of God Is Within You.* Nyack, N.Y.: Fellowship Publications.

Sharp, Gene. *The Politics of Nonviolent Action,* Porter Sargent Publisher, 11 Beacon St., Boston, Mass.

THE CHRISTIAN IDEAL OF NON-VIOLENCE

American Friends Service Committee. *The Draft.* New York: Hill & Wang, 1968. This is a very good summary of the history of the draft, its effect, and the way it works.

Bainton, Roland. *Christian Attitudes Towards War and Peace.* New York: Abingdon Press, 1960, paper.

Douglas, James. *The Non-violent Cross.* New York: Macmillan. 1968.

Lasserre, Jean. *War and the Gospel.* Herald Press, Scotsdale, Pa., 1962.

Kaufman, Donald D. *What Belongs to Caesar,* Herald Press, Scotsdale, Pa.

Macgregor, G. *The New Testament Basis of Pacifism.* Nyack, N.Y.: Fellowship Publications, 1966, paper.

Merton, Thomas. *Faith and Violence.* University of Notre Dame Press, 1968, paper.

Orr, Edgar. *Christian Pacifism.* C.W. Daniel Co., Ashingdon, 1958.

Reganey, P. *Non-violence and the Christian Conscience.* New York: Herder and Herder, 1966.

ECONOMICS OF WAR: THE MILITARY-INDUSTRIAL COMPLEX

Barnet, Richard J. *The Economy of Death.* New York: Anthenaeum, 1969.

Coffin, Tristam. *The Armed Society: Militarism in Modern America.* Baltimore: Pelican Books, 1964.

Lens, Sidney. *The Day Before Doomsday.* Doubleday, 1977.

Lens, Sidney. *The Military Industrial Complex,* Pilgrim Press and the National Catholic Reporter, 1970.

McCormick, Rory. *Americans Against Man.* Washington, Corpus, 1970.

Melman, Seymour. *The Permanent War Economy,* Simon Schuster, 1974.

Swomley, John. *The Military Establishment.* Boston: Beacon Press, 1964.

VIETNAM

Fall, Bernard, *The Two Vietnams: A Political and Military Analysis,* New York: Praeger, 1965.

Gettleman, Marvin (ed.) *Vietnam: History, Documents and Opinions on a Major World Crisis.* Greenwich, Conn.: Fawcett, 1965.

Harvey, Frank. *Airwar Vietnam.* New York: Bantam, 1967, paper.

PROCESS OF PEACE

Berrigan, Daniel, *No Bars to Manhood,* Bantam Books, 1970.

Berrigan, Philip. *Punishment for Peace.* New York: Macmillan, 1969.

Breakthrough to Peace: *12 Views on the Threat of Thermonuclear Extermination* (intro. by Thomas Merton). New York: New Directions, 1962, paper.

King, Martin Luther. *Where Do We Go from Here? Chaos or Community?* New York: Harper & Row, 1966.

Merton, Thomas. *Thomas Merton on Peace.* McCall, N.Y., 1971.

Myrdal, Alva. *How the United States and Russia Run the Arms Race.* New York: Pantheon Books.

Prasad, Devi (ed.) *Grandam, the Land Revolution in India.* War Resisters International, 3 Caledonia Road, London, N.1., England.

United Nations Association of the USA. *Controlling Conflicts in the 1970's.* UN Association, 833 UN Plaza, N.Y., 1969.

United Nations Association of the USA. *Stopping the Spread of Nuclear Weapons,* 1967.

HISTORY OF PACIFISM

Brock, Peter. *Pacifism in the United States,* Princeton University Press, 1968.

Almost all of these books contain bibliographies which afford the opportunity for wider reading.